C.E.O.
SATISFACTION

C.E.O.
SATISFACTION

DON DUFORD

Columbus, Ohio

C.E.O Satisfaction
Published by Gatekeeper Press
3971 Hoover Rd. Suite 77
Columbus, OH 43123-2839

www.GatekeeperPress.com

Copyright © 2017 by Don Duford

All rights reserved. Neither this book, nor any parts within it may be sold or reproduced in any form or by any electronic or mechanical means, including information storage and retrieval systems without permission in writing from the author. The only exception is by a reviewer, who may quote short excerpts in a review.

ISBN: 9781619847026

Printed in the United States of America

Contents

Introduction 1

Chapter 1: C.E.O. Satisfaction 7

Chapter 2: What is C.E.O. Satisfaction? 11

Chapter 3: People, People, People 25

Chapter 4: Defining Satisfaction for Customers 35

Chapter 5: Defining Satisfaction for Employees 45

Chapter 6: Defining Satisfaction for Owners 65

Chapter 7: Finding and Maintaining Balance 79

Chapter 8: Becoming a C.E.O. Satisfier 93

Final Thoughts 113

Introduction

ROBERT HUGHES, THE president and chief executive officer of Progressive Industries, took the podium at his retirement dinner. He stood before hundreds of employees, customers, and members of the board of directors, and paused before speaking as a hush fell over the ballroom.

After a few moments, he broke the silence.

"Forty-three years ago, we were a successful but small company in a small but successful city, employing just over 300 people. We made bearings for the automotive industry. Back then we knew what only a handful of industry insiders knew: that we made the best damn bearings in the world."

The cheers that erupted were not just for his words; they were for him.

He continued: "And we've been committed to sustained success for so many years and through so many cycles in the market because..." Hughes paused for dramatic effect. "Because we've always been about our customers. They, and we, went through all the good times and the bad times the market cycles brought us, and we did it together.

"Let's go back to the bad old days for a moment, to the 1970s, when the auto industry was in transition. The country was coming out of its first energy crisis, and our customers—

the American car makers who have been with us through thick and thin—realized that for the first time, they had competition from overseas. Europeans were making better luxury cars, the Japanese were making better economy cars, and our American customers were stuck in the middle. Our auto industry was making cars based on marketing and manufacturing strategies that were on the way out, but few people knew it then. The good news for us is that a good number of the people who saw these changes were here at Progressive. We saw what Ford, GM, and Chrysler needed to do because they were our customers, and we *listened* when they talked about the threats they saw. Some of you here tonight will remember the turmoil of those years and how some of our best friend in the auto industry suddenly found themselves out of a job. And these people were our *real customers*, and their problems hit home with us.

"But even when these good people couldn't rely on their long-time employers, we at Progressive recognized their talents and skills, and we stuck with them. We got through tough times together because we found ways to help one other. One of these individuals comes to mind, and he's here with us tonight. Frank Johnson, can you please stand up for a moment?"

Mr. Johnson dutifully complied and received light applause.

"Now, in the 1970s, Frank had a successful career with the Pontiac Division of General Motors; he and his engineers had designed some of the most reliable drive trains in the business. But when the oil shock hit and cars got smaller, Pontiac thought Frank's time had come and gone, and Frank was soon out of a job. Frank, of course, never gave up: he let me know he was already looking for work and that when he found it, he'd be coming to us for bearings and other products. And I believed him.

"Three months later, Frank got in touch and asked me to write him a letter of recommendation for a position at Ford, which I did gladly. He visited us when he got the job, and I'll never forget what he said: 'Bob, I've always been able to trust Progressive's products. So today, I'm here to ask you to work with us to help make our next generation of automobiles competitive throughout the world.' Frank believed he had found the secret to Ford's future success, and he shared it with us. 'There's one way we're going to succeed together,' he said, 'and that's by focusing on *quality*.'

"Frank needed products that would help him succeed at Ford, and elsewhere, so we all bought into the idea of improving quality even further. But then some of our core employees here realized that we couldn't simply make the best bearings anymore if we wanted to grow exponentially. We had to expand our product lines, they said, we had to bring our level of quality to other automotive parts.

"This process of improvement and expansion had crystalized when we asked ourselves why international car makers were taking over the U.S. market. It wasn't market differentiation, fuel efficiency, or new assembly lines. It was just what Frank had said: *quality*. That seems obvious now. But the American auto industry was built on planned obsolescence."

Hughes clicked the remote, and on the screen behind him appeared photographs of some of Detroit's most beautiful automobiles from the 1950s, '60s, and '70s—all of them full of color, chrome, and style.

"Every year, new designs masked the fact that cars would rust out, engine blocks would fail, and transmissions weren't built to last forever. But the industry kept consumers' minds off that by rolling out bigger engines, and faster cars. People weren't mad that their cars needed an overhaul. Instead, they saw the shiny new models on TV, and they wanted them. It was a perfect gravy train, and, frankly, we were all on it.

"But that gravy train wasn't going to run much longer.

Customers suddenly didn't want bigger engines. They wanted better, more efficient, more *reliable* engines. They wanted a car they could own for years to come. This was good for us: we made the best bearings in the world. A marketplace focused on quality was coming our way. At the beginning, we weren't sure where our customers were going to go, and frankly neither were they, but we had spent years engaging in genuine dialogue with our customers, and we got real, honest information from them about how to grow our business."

"Of course, we didn't just communicate with our *customers*; we also listened to our *employees*. When we saw quality as a growing competitive advantage, we talked about how to make things even better. Our bearings were always outlasting the cars they were in, but we needed to make sure this would still be true if cars lasted ten years, not five. We needed to make sure quality would remain a key brand identifier, and so we challenged our engineering and manufacturing departments to find ways to make that happen. And they did. We made our bearings even better.

"Then in the late 1970's our employees came up with an idea that transformed our company. They said that since we had already made the best bearings even better, why not expand our line, create more great parts for more auto makers? Capture more of the market with the customer we already have. Well, that was a big step, and frankly, a scary one. But in the end, we listened. And acted.

"So by 1980 we were no longer Progressive Bearings. To keep up with expanding automotive parts lines, we became Progressive Industries. Our board and our investors committed millions of dollars to retooling and new plant construction. Our sales were growing—our reputation for quality had gained us so much loyalty that our expanded product lines were being snapped up my auto manufacturers at an astonishing rate.

"But is always comes back to people, doesn't it? To our customers, employees, and owners, right? Back in the 1970s, some remarkable people began their careers here at Progressive, some of them right out of high school. We always saw the value of being loyal to our employees, of giving them an opportunity to succeed, because loyalty is a two-way street. In fact, there are several of you here tonight who got so good at what you did that you were recruited by other companies; some of you even became presidents of your own companies. Tonight we thank you for all you've contributed to our company, both while you were here and in your new roles as trusted business partners. The fact is that employees are just as important as our customers. Employees, like customers, are people. And we've all learned that in good times or bad, people are ultimately all we have. The good news is that the people at Progressive are all we need.

"And that brings us to the third group of people responsible for the success we're celebrating tonight: *the owners*. They found partners to add to their investments as the company grew, and they found the private equity partners that taught us how to acquire complementary businesses and help us grow our lines.

"Of course, it wasn't always easy. Black Monday in 1987, the tech bubble crash of 2000, and the Great Recession in 2008 all took their toll. We laid off some of our workers and took a beating in our company valuation. Those were painful times, but they taught us a lot and helped us prepare for the next crisis. For example, when our largest competitor decided to go after us by dropping their prices by ten percent, we lost customers. We had to scale back on raises and benefits for a time. But through it all, our employees and owners took care of one another, all while staying true to our commitment to quality. Eventually we won back our customers.

"Today, we stay attuned to market trends, and we keep our

manufacturing processes as lean as possible so we can adjust quickly. We're ready for future challenges in the same way we were ready for the changes in the 1970s. We listen. We pay attention to what our customers want. We listen to and work with our employees, and we communicate with our board and shareholders. They trust us to make sound business decisions, and our customers trust us as well."

Hughes's voice cracked a little as he clicked through a series of corporate logos dating back to the 1970s. "It's that trust that kept us successful in the past and will keep us successful in the future. Tonight, I share with you the appreciation and pride I will always feel for the forty-three years I've been a part of Progressive Industries."

CHAPTER 1

C.E.O. Satisfaction

THE STORY OF Robert Hughes and Progressive Global Industries, though fictional, is based on real events, trends, benefits, and results that can be achieved by implementing the ideas of what I call C.E.O. Satisfaction.

Robert Hughes was a successful CEO because he practiced C.E.O. Satisfaction and addressed the needs of the three core groups found in any business: customers, employees, and owners.

Leading an organization requires many different skills. For example, a business manager can achieve noteworthy success by being a marketing whiz or by designing the best manufacturing process in the industry. Truly great success, however, is achieved by ensuring that the organization's customers, employees, and owners are all satisfied. Technical and functional achievements bolster a business's success only if those achievements continually strengthen the commitment of all three core groups. It's very easy for one area of a company to unintentionally erode another.

Of course, a leader may need to make decisions that will

temporarily upset the balance between the three stakeholder groups. This is when C.E.O. satisfaction is most critical, as decisions that address only the current crisis and do not consider the stakeholders could prove to be devastating and might take years to correct.

C.E.O. Satisfaction is a never-ending balancing act, but when it becomes part of an overall leadership style, it earns an invaluable reward: trust.

C.E.O. SATISFACTION: A UNIQUE SET OF STRATEGIC SKILLS FOR EFFECTIVE LEADERSHIP

Many experienced executives believe a successful leader needs to "think like a CEO." This cliché is often followed by recommendations for hiring the best people, practicing a certain management style, setting goals, and creating compensation packages.

Instead of thinking *like* a CEO, I invite readers to think *about* the C, E, and O: the customers, employees, and owners. Specifically, the real competency behind "thinking like a CEO" is *accountable strategic agility,* and "thinking about the C., E., and O." creates accountable strategic agility. Best of all, you can develop and apply these concepts whether you are a CEO or an assistant manager. Using your current work environment, you have access to a learning laboratory where you can learn and put into practice the C.E.O. skills that will make you an effective leader. No matter where you are on the corporate ladder, if you look around, you will see customers, employees, and owners. You can observe them, learn about their fundamental needs, and create strategies for satisfying each group. In fact, learning to understand what satisfies those around you is the key to excelling throughout your career.

Regardless of your job title, there will always be customers, employees, and owners around you, and each group will have skills, needs, and ideas that you can practice engaging and satisfying. The things you do to satisfy your first few customers can teach you something about satisfying your future customers; similarly, the way you satisfy your first two employees will hone your skills for managing two hundred or two thousand later. Learning how to satisfy the goals of the owners in your first position will give you insights into how to successfully manage your relationships with a board of directors.

Thinking *about* the C.E.O. instead of thinking *like* a CEO is not a difficult transition to make. Doing so will help you understand the organization and your place in it. It will require effort, but thinking about the C.E.O. will bring about many new opportunities as you learn to satisfy all three stakeholder groups.

This is the premise of this book. The C.E.O. Satisfaction methodology has worked for me. Its principles have allowed me to create real opportunities for the customers, employees, and owners I've worked with, all while remaining true to myself. I invite you to consider how the principles in this book will allow you to do the same. Hopefully, you'll find that they can guide your career development in a more effective way than you may have thought possible.

In the following chapters, I'll present a game plan to help you develop from an average manager to what I call an NEO (a *newly emerging orchestrator* of the C.E.O. methodology) to a full C.E.O Satisfaction practitioner. First, we'll discuss a few fundamental things:

- The C.E.O. Satisfaction philosophy
- The importance of recognizing basic human nature in a work setting

Next, we'll build the framework for developing your C.E.O. satisfaction radar:

- Understanding what satisfies customers, employees, and owners
- Understanding how to balance your development by exploring Paradoxical Pairs

Finally, we'll tackle putting the concepts into action:

- Defining your Sphere of Influence
- Using the CorePlus planning tool

Whether or not you ever become a CEO, you'll earn the trust and respect of your Cs, Es, and Os by using the C.E.O. Satisfaction Methodology. When you do, you'll satisfy one other important stakeholder: you!

CHAPTER 2

What is C.E.O. Satisfaction?

C USTOMERS. EMPLOYEES. OWNERS.
These are the three most important stakeholder groups to satisfy. In this chapter, we'll take a look at who they are, what they need, and how their needs can be satisfied. We won't consider one group over another; instead, all three should be considered at the same time. It's a challenging balancing act, to be sure. But it's also a rewarding challenge—one that, when met, announces that you have arrived. What do I mean by that? Look around. There are customers, employees, and owners in your organization. These three stakeholder groups were here last year, ten years ago, and fifty years ago. They're here today, and they'll be here years after you retire. Satisfying these groups and communicating with them effectively means that you've opened the door, that you have the tools and skillset to successfully manage a business. That you're ready.

I developed the concept of C.E.O. Satisfaction after reviewing my career and the careers of others. Hopefully you can use the concepts and tools in this book to develop your C.E.O. skills and propel your own career.

There were two "aha moments" in my career that helped crystallize the C.E.O. Satisfaction approach. One was on my first day as president and CEO of a business, when the first-hand experience of being responsible for an entire organization hit me in a way I couldn't have predicted. The second occurred years later, during the first days of my role as president/CEO of another company. The new director of human resources had asked me what skills had enabled me to become a leader. Although each of these moments occurred when I was a new CEO, the real aha came from reflecting on the years before.

I realized that my approach to leadership had been formed while I held various junior positions in the companies where I worked. I learned by working with the people around me, communicating with them, and finding ways to satisfy them and appreciating the importance of alignment. That's the beauty of the C.E.O. Satisfaction approach: you can practice it at any point in your career, and the earlier the better. Remembering to make the effort to understand the needs of the people in your key stakeholder groups, to develop ways to satisfy their needs, and to grasp the importance of keeping the satisfaction of those around you in balance is the essence of C.E.O. Satisfaction. Customers, employees, and owners are the primary stakeholders in any business, and focusing on them and their alignment creates a methodology that can be shared with others. However, the important thing to remember about customers, employees, and owners is that they are all people. Conceptual categories are fine for thinking and developing strategies and plans. But management—and leadership—is the practice of understanding and satisfying *people*.

MY FIRST AHA MOMENT

My first day in my first president/CEO position was, understandably, a memorable one. On that day, I gained one of the most important insights about my professional career. Prior to that day, my focus had been on demonstrating my capabilities so that I would gain recognition among my superiors and receive promotions. Until I became CEO, I was, of course, primarily focused on keeping my boss happy. Or, to be more accurate, I was focused on keeping a succession of bosses happy.

Demonstrating my capabilities generally involved focusing on my department's achievements or on the management of a project. In other words, I was looking at the trees and not at the forest.

On that first day as president/CEO, I experienced the change in perspective that came with this senior role. I was responsible for the entire organization, and ensuring its success required a balanced and objective view of the all of the pieces in it. No longer did I have *my* department or *my* projects. Instead, the entire company was my business. I was surprised at how this new vantage point changed my perspective. I thought I had always taken a holistic view of situations at work. Now, I considered the entire company as a whole: it was a collection of teams, each with its own goals and needs, and they were all depending on me to create a system that satisfied those needs. Suddenly, my interest in IT, billing/collections, and risk management was equal to my interest in sales/marketing and human resources. Just a few days prior, I focused most of time on my department alone.

Additionally, I now was responsible for leading the internal corporate culture, which included everyone from the most junior employees to my senior team, as well as the company's external brand as it needed to be expressed to customers, advisors, the press, and even government officials. And, of course, the owners who gave me the responsibility of managing their investments were expecting improving returns. This first aha moment taught me that I was now responsible for the entire forest *and* the health of each and every tree in it.

The importance of alignment over the focused achievement of one unit—in other words, the difference between being responsible for the forest and not just my trees—became clear almost immediately. In one of the positions I held just before assuming my role as president/CEO, I was responsible for the company's sales, marketing, and product development functions. In this role, I would constantly challenge our technology group to build and implement unique solutions for our biggest clients in order to maintain good relationships and keep our monthly sales on target. These were key goals for me and my team. In response to my challenges, our IT leader became concerned that her employees were growing frustrated with customer expectations. They wound up having to work long hours and experienced less satisfaction on the job. At the same time, our CFO, who was focused on owner satisfaction, would challenge me to concentrate the sales team's efforts on collections and pricing issues; he was concerned about a trend in receivables that could become a liability to our financial performance. In my role as director of sales and marketing, I understood that these were real and important issues, and I worked with both the IT leader and the CFO to reach a solution. But because my goals were related to growth, I always operated with a bias to get my sales team the technology tools we needed and to minimize efforts in collections. I processed everything through my own filter and kept my sights on what would best demonstrate my capabilities as a sales and marketing director and keep my boss happy.

Once I became president/CEO, I began operating more

objectively. I listened to—and engaged with—all of my department heads more empathetically, because their challenges were the organization's challenges, and therefore they were my challenges, too. The directions we pursued needed to be more balanced: we needed to consider our customers, employees, and owners. As a result, our overall performance improved. This same type of learning experience—when my new vantage point made it clear why alignment is so critical and how elusive this alignment can be given the different demands of individual departments and functional units—has continued throughout my career.

Organizational alignment can occur only when everyone in the business understands the organization's goals and the unique role each person plays in accomplishing those goals. Early on in my career, I was fortunate to work at company whose culture emphasized developing potential leaders. A key element of that culture was diversifying learning through rotational assignments. In this environment, I learned to be comfortable with making myself expendable and my team self-sustaining. Put another way, it became my goal to make sure the business unit I led would continue to succeed on its own after I'd moved on. This approach made delegation an essential element of my managerial philosophy, and when I became CEO later on, my delegation skills kept me from trying to take control of every aspect of the business. It led me to develop the people skills and insights necessary to listen to the needs of the people responsible for managing their "trees" in order for us to share the benefits of a successful forest. Being a leader that enabled performance—rather than enforced performance—led me to implement the C.E.O. Satisfaction model described in this book.

When I became a president/CEO, I no longer had the luxury of focusing on just one part of the organization. I needed to ensure that the entire organization was aligned so that we could achieve our company-wide strategic objectives. My first big aha moment as CEO came when I understood that looking at issues, people, opportunities, and challenges requires a unique perspective—one that highlights the importance and challenges of finding and maintaining alignment among stakeholders. It also confirmed once and for all the importance of understanding Cs, Es, and Os.

MY SECOND AHA MOMENT

This aha moment happened a few years later, during my time as president/CEO of a different company. I was meeting with a human resources executive responsible for talent development, and we were discussing ways to accelerate the growth of future leaders. She asked what had enabled me to grow and develop into a leader. At the time, I struggled with my answer. I did not consider my starting point in business to have been advantaged. After being the first person in my lower-middle-class family to attend college—a small state college, for the record—I began my business career as an average management trainee. My communication skills were not outstanding early in my career, and I was not highly competitive, super intelligent, great at networking, or very skilled in any specific business discipline. Many of my colleagues had much stronger "classic" business skills, but they didn't become top leaders like I did. Why? What did I do differently? Was it just luck? At the time, I thought it might have been because I had worked a little harder or had gotten lucky with my early assignments and developed skills that would benefit me later on. I did feel that my ability to define a team's goal, organize the team, and delegate responsibility might have been a personal differentiator. And I was always comfortable with people.

After much contemplation, I realized that my path to the top was largely driven by what I now call the C.E.O. Satisfaction approach. Though I wasn't fully aware of it at the time, it was this C.E.O. Satisfaction approach that gave me the confidence to take on tough assignments, accelerate my learning as a leader, and to differentiate myself from my peers. My first aha moment made me aware of my broad organizational responsibility, and I was well prepared to accept and excel at these responsibilities because of the C.E.O. Satisfaction approach I had consistently employed in my previous roles.

Using the C.E.O. Satisfaction approach meant that I viewed every assignment as if I were my own boss. I respected and supported the people I worked for—the people who entrusted me with the assignment. I clearly understood what my superiors needed from me, but I always set bigger, broader goals for myself. I learned to set specific timeframes—monthly, quarterly, annually—to measure how well I had accomplished each goal. Frequently, these goals had no impact on my formal performance evaluations. At times, my performance reviews were average while my personal accomplishments were very good; at other times, things were the other way around. Creating my own standards for evaluating my job performance, and contrasting these with my formal performance reviews, helped me understand that annual reviews drive near-term achievements and compensation decisions while personal goals drive career development.

For example, a few of the positions I held in the early stages of my career involved running regional customer service operations. The standard measures of performance for these departments usually involved team productivity and expense control, along with simple, measurable service targets like processing time. These simple targets made sense because they were quantifiable, easy to collect, and consistent across the entire network of service operations. One of these operations—a small one I ran in Cincinnati—was performing poorly when I arrived. It took three years, but the operation eventually tripled in size and became the preferred service site for many of the company's largest clients. Ironically, during the transformation, we did not excel in the basic targets: we were usually right on them, or maybe even a little below. My goals for myself and my team included meeting the basic targets, but, more importantly, we set additional targets for ourselves in customer satisfaction and people development. The customer satisfaction targets came from working with our clients and our account managers. For example, if the company standard for processing time was five days, but we knew some of our customers needed certain transactions to be handled differently, we figured out how to align our transactions with their internal business needs. At times, this hurt our internal average processing times, but it forged strong partnerships with our clients.

In order to support the operation's transformation, I understood the need to strengthen the skills and abilities of the management team. I set personal goals for each of them that began with simply increasing basic supervisory skills. Eventually, I selected a few to be senior leaders and helped develop their skills even further. We also established continuity by creating a bench of qualified internal candidates for all key positions on the team. As a result of our team's efforts, our company was rewarded with increased business from existing clients and strong references for potential new clients. None of those activities counted in my performance assessment with my boss, but they were critical in my self-assessment. We simply took a larger view of our operation than what was required by our boss by adding ways to measure and improve our customer satisfaction and by providing on-the-job satisfaction for employees. By setting targets to increase customer satisfaction, strengthen management, and increase productivity, I was, in fact, practicing an early version of C.E.O. Satisfaction. The model served me well then, and it continued to serve me well when I led an entire company.

How did I do it? There are many strategies for assessing a customer's needs and satisfaction. Similarly, there are several strategies you can use to satisfy employees. Owner interests are also fairly clear: they like steady, predictable, and profitable growth. Most of the strategies business leaders use to satisfy customers, employees, and owners are effective and well designed. They can be learned in school, from a book, or from a mentor. The C.E.O. Satisfaction approach focuses on balancing the strategies used to satisfy each of the three stakeholder groups. The goal of the C.E.O. Satisfaction approach is to minimize "either/or" strategies and create more "and" strategies.

ALIGNMENT, ASSESSMENT, ACHIEVEMENT: THE CONSTANTS OF C.E.O. SATISFACTION

Maintaining balance is a concept that cannot be overemphasized. Business leaders frequently allow the interests of only one of the three stakeholder groups to drive the decision-making process. These interests are generally very specific to a single group, and their measurements of success do not translate well to the other groups.

Equally problematic, these individual groups often employ strategies that are oriented toward short-term results. You've probably practiced or learned about a number of different techniques designed to improve a business's performance with one of the three key groups. There are growth initiatives to attract more customers, human-capital initiatives to motivate employees, and expense-reduction initiatives to lower corporate spending. The longer your career, the more times you'll see "best practices" like these come and go. If you've been in business as long as I have, you'll also know that some of these practices always beat out others. For example, human-capital programs and investments in growth and infrastructure are usually the first casualties of expense-reduction initiatives; conversely, in times of expansion, companies often primarily invest in programs designed to grow sales and market share.

As a result, the behavior of an organization can be a series of mood swings instead of a firm commitment to a balanced alignment. C.E.O. Satisfaction, on the other hand, emphasizes balancing the competing priorities of the three stakeholder groups and maintaining that balance over time. Consistent efforts aimed at larger, long-term goals assure stakeholders that their leaders have a clear vision of the future of the organization and know how to maintain programs that will achieve goals over time.

But balance doesn't mean equilibrium; it means maintaining alignment. There are times when a business needs to focus heavily on market, competition, or efficiency issues. These are times when the C.E.O. Satisfaction approach is most critical.

If the crisis involves employee recruitment and retention, the CEO will likely tell the HR leader to solve the problem. If the crisis involves customer retention or acquisition, the sales/marketing leader will be tasked to solve it. And if it's a profitability crisis, the CFO will get the "solve it" assignment. In each case, a solution will be found, but if the leader is not versed in C.E.O. Satisfaction thinking, an effective short-term solution can cause dissatisfaction among other stakeholders, ultimately resulting in cyclical crisis management. Sometimes one stakeholder group can be so loud that you overlook a quieter one. We'll discuss this further when we address each stakeholder.

Maintaining alignment among customers, employees, and owners is only possible if you are skilled at assessing the satisfaction for each. Business schools, books, and consulting firms all provide strategies for assessing satisfaction, and the C.E.O. satisfaction model works in tandem with them. The key is that a C.E.O. leader will interpret customer, employee, and owner satisfaction differently than the "solve the problem" leader will, and will therefore plan a different—and more successful—course of action.

Every business is unique, but I believe that there are a few fundamental strategies for satisfying customers, employees, and owners that are applicable in almost any business. Other strategies may be specific to only one business. The important thing is to ensure the basic strategies are in place before you create others.

"Alignment" and "assessment" can sound overly conceptual, which is why "achievement" is critical. The C.E.O. Satisfaction approach is not only a mindset; it's a call to action. Maintaining satisfaction and avoiding disruption are what ultimately makes the approach valuable. It's about setting goals and meeting them, even while fighting the fires that inevitably ignite every week.

The skills needed to keep the accelerator down on long-term efforts to improve C.E.O. Satisfaction while successfully delivering on near-term objectives can be developed through what I call the CorePlus planning model. Early on in your career, you won't have access to all the levers that a leader has at his or her disposal. Instead, you'll have a boss who has been tasked with solving a problem, and he or she will tell you what that solution will be and how you'll be involved in enacting it. Still, it's never too early to start practicing the C.E.O. methodology. In the early stages of your career, the CorePlus approach—which we'll discuss later as well—is a good way to satisfy your boss while also being creative in addressing the need for balance among the three stakeholder groups.

For now, here is a simple introduction to the CorePlus concept: In addition to the objectives required by your job (the "core"), you task yourself with three to five additional objectives (the "plus" goals) that relate to customer, employee, and owner satisfaction. They must be measurable and have a time limit. If your core responsibilities directly contribute to the satisfaction of one of the three stakeholder groups, then your plus goals should focus on the other two. As a practitioner of the CorePlus approach, you will look to the customers, employees, and owners and determine what you think is necessary to succeed in your job on your own terms. The plus goals you set for yourself will define your relationship with the three key stakeholder groups and will ultimately be more important than your core requirements. But remember that it's always CorePlus, not "Core or Plus." You need to satisfy your supervisor by meeting core requirements first. CorePlus requires extra effort, but it's well worth it.

TWO FINAL POINTS

I developed the C.E.O. Satisfaction model over the last forty years. My career started when business was very high touch/low tech and ended in an era of increasingly high tech/low touch. So, I questioned if these concepts still make sense, and I've concluded that they absolutely do. Most businesses still use a traditional model: they depend on employees and investors to serve customers and support their strategies, respectively. You may think that the net-based economy would change that, but at the end of the day, businesses that distribute a product or service rely heavily on their customers, employees, and owners. Amazon employs tens of thousands of people, as does Apple and Google. More and more businesses depend on independent contractors to deliver a service—for example, Uber does this—so the definition of "employee" may change, but the idea of satisfying employees is still the same. There are "new" models, such as the one used by Facebook, that rely on capturing "eyeballs" and selling access to those eyeballs to generate revenue. I put quotations around the word "new" because the old media businesses—newspapers and magazines—are essentially the same, although the definition of customer is a little different. Unless you're the genius or marketer who created the concepts that built these businesses, you need to develop an experiential development plan to enable yourself to run one of these businesses. The C.E.O. Satisfaction approach can work for you.

Another foundational concept in C.E.O. Satisfaction is one we've already mentioned, and it's one we'll revisit in Chapter 3: customers, owners, and employees are first and foremost human beings, and they cannot be part of a successful team unless their fundamental human nature is considered. Their needs must to be identified and understood, and the things that satisfy them need to be considered and evaluated. Thinking of stakeholders as people—instead of as impersonal categories—is a critical element in the C.E.O. Satisfaction philosophy.

CHAPTER 3

People, People, People

We all know that the three most valuable things about a real estate asset are "location, location, location." The most valuable things about a business are "people, people, people." Underlying the philosophy of C.E.O. Satisfaction is the premise that all business dynamics—interactions with customers, employees, and owners—are the result of people making decisions and taking actions. These actions are based on human needs, which can be understood and managed through preparation and analysis. Think of any scenario for problem solving, creativity, execution, market growth, etc that occurs every day in businesses. We can all come up with examples of people acting together or in conflict to solve or create a business problem. Every action, every decision, every relationship ultimately comes down to a human being deciding to do something, or deciding not to do something, in a world of other human beings. Leadership is the science and practice of identifying the actions that would most likely lead to an organization's success and then doing what it takes to make those actions happen. In short, success in a corporate setting means communicating with, motivating, and aligning individual people in order to reach a shared goal. Success also requires engaged participants, and that engagement requires trust.

We'll address assessing satisfiers for each of the three stakeholder groups later. For now, it's just important to acknowledge and understand that all of a business's techniques, strategies, and programs are really behavior-modification efforts: urging customers to buy more, employees to improve absenteeism, investors to keep investing, and so on. If you can understand this, you'll make more deep and insightful decisions. You'll avoid thinking of critical groups of people—hourly workers, for example—as impersonal segments of a business model. The people in your sphere of influence will appreciate and admire your thoughtful decision making, and you will engender trust.

CUSTOMERS AS PEOPLE

For starters, let's look at customers and the things they do that a business might seek to influence: using a product for the first time, purchasing a replacement product, canceling a purchase, or upgrading a purchase. Customers are generally individuals and they make purchases to meet their personal needs. They can be segmented into groups by age, sex, marital status, income, education, and so forth. Understanding what humans do in a consumer- and product-based world can be achieved by studying the discreet actions of a series of individuals. Each individual consumer acts on a unique set of buying criteria, and a business succeeds when it is able to influence many individuals to make similar purchase decisions. Tools like advertising, product placement, and pricing strategies all come into play as a business seeks to increase sales. In addition to using these tools, I urge you to think about your customers as humans. You probably know people in your family or community circles who match the target customer profiles derived from research. Seek these individuals out and talk to them to learn firsthand how the assumptions in the marketing findings match each individual's perspective—and how they don't. After several of these interactions, you'll learn how the marketing assumptions fit—and how they don't. This insight will help you interpret future research findings more effectively.

But what about the B2B world? As it turns out, the same principles are at work. Of course, the business customer is basing purchasing decisions on organizational criteria—a more complicated collection of interests and needs. You might think that business customers don't fit into the people discussion I just laid out. After all, business customers follow the company's purchasing guidelines and often work in teams. However, the individual people involved in business purchasing are doing a job, a job they hope their company will recognize and reward them for doing well. They take a risk every time they make a purchasing recommendation. If you understand this and can meet their personal needs—in addition to their purchasing criteria—you will engender their trust and confidence, giving you a strong competitive advantage. Get to know your business customers—understand them as both people *and* as representatives of their businesses—and your decision-making processes will improve. More often than not, you'll also wind up keeping customers longer. Meeting customers on a regular basis is a terrific way to learn about the human behavioral aspects of the sales process. Best of all, what you'll learn from these interactions is nearly impossible to forget.

In Chapter 6, we'll take a detailed look at satisfying business customers. But for now, we'll focus on the individual customers and how they respond to your efforts to sell to them. Ultimately, a successful brand is built by the market's perception of your performance. After all, the market is a composite of the many human beings who have responded favorably to your sales efforts. They are either individuals or businesses who have been influenced by your efforts, and they're ready to make a repeat or initial purchase.

Understanding customers as free individuals, or as organized stakeholder groups in other businesses, and meeting their needs better than your competitors will differentiate your business and create brand value. More importantly, this process creates a brand built on trust. Trust has always been the critical driver of brand differentiation. In fact, because of the myriad of social media sites that collect and distribute opinions and customer reviews, trust might be the *only* driver.

EMPLOYEES AS PEOPLE

The role of humans in employee satisfaction may seem obvious. Employees are humans, and there are plenty of existing strategies for keeping them happy and productive—or, as some experts put it: "maximizing human capital." I tend to think of companies as dynamic organisms composed of interdependent webs in which each employee has a unique and integral role. Actually, two roles. First, each employee does a particular job that's described in the Responsibilities section of a job description. Second, through social interactions in the workplace, the employee has an impact on the effectiveness of other employees, who are unique and integral elements of this living organism and have the same two roles. The collective actions of an organization's employees influence—for better or worse—the effectiveness and performance of the company as a whole. Employees either add to or subtract from the company's ability to meet the needs of the customers and achieve the goals laid out by the owners. While some employees clearly have more impact than others do, every employee has a contribution to make. And sometimes, the value of certain employees' contributions may be under recognized. For example, front-line service people often have the most influence on the way a customer perceives the company; however, they frequently receive less consideration than the vice president of sales does.

Employees want to be—and need to be—understood as unique individuals; they don't want to be grouped into larger categories. Sustainable employee satisfaction, therefore, does not come from fun activities and perks. At the end of the day, everyone wants to be valued and respected. Everyone would like to go home at night with a sense of accomplishment, and everyone wants to know he or she has an opportunity to learn and grow while performing his or her job. Some business terminology refers to this level of employee satisfaction as engagement, but regardless of what it is called, this sense of accomplishment, of being valued, of having opportunities to learn and grow on the job, of being part of a successful team, creates a core foundation of *trust*. Satisfied employees trust that their employer will treat them fairly, keep them informed, and value them. They spend most of their waking hours at work, so it's reasonable to see the workplace as a community designed by its leaders to treat them well, give them opportunities, and maybe have some fun along the way.

It's never too early to practice the kinds of interactions that lead to mutual understanding, teamwork, and trust. NEOs, particularly those who work in large organizations, engage in multiple interactions on a daily basis. Making these interactions as positive and productive as possible is great way to develop what some people sometimes call the "business feel."

In my opinion, the business feel is really just the sum of years of practice listening to colleagues, co-workers, customers, and bosses, and learning what satisfies and dissatisfies them. Interacting with colleagues is one of the many ways the workplace can teach you something no educational institution can.

OWNERS AS PEOPLE

Finally, let's consider the company's owners. It's pretty straightforward; these are individuals investing money in the business. In some cases, they are passive investor institutions: for example, the owners and managers of mutual funds. In other cases, the owners are very active investors; perhaps they are private equity firms, joint venture managers, or even "angel" investors who want to participate in managerial decisions. In all cases, owners are seeking a return on investment, but the particulars differ from individual to individual. Some want long-term payouts; others are looking for short-term returns. Similar to customers, owners use a number of technical criteria to guide their decisions. But at the end of the day, they want to trust that the people running the company know what to do, will design solid strategies and plans, and will execute these plans successfully.

When judging a company's performance, owners typically focus their attention on management. But good management is ultimately based on the ability to engage employees and create a unique brand that will attract and retain customers. A common challenge in achieving owner satisfaction is related to profitability. Generally, profits are forecast, reported, and interpreted as measures of success over a limited time—usually quarterly, but sometimes monthly or annually. Conversely, the C.E.O. Satisfaction philosophy states that business leaders will not allow short-term gains to outweigh long-term, sustainable performance. Since owners actually own the business and have the authority to make the final decisions, this is not always an easy thing to accomplish; we will discuss this in more detail later.

I've been asked if, in the C.E.O. methodology, "owners" can be replaced by "bosses." Is keeping a boss happy good practice for keeping an owner happy? My answer is a firm no. While it's true that bosses are superior to their subordinates and that owners are superior to executives, this is where the similarity ends. Bosses are ultimately employees: they're trying to succeed just like everyone else. Your boss likely reports to his or her boss, who, in turn, reports to another boss. Bosses, therefore, are motivated by satisfying their own bosses. Owners, on the other hand, are satisfied by financial returns on investments. In fact, bosses often see their own needs as being more important than the owners' needs. Therefore, focusing on satisfying your boss without thinking about the company's owners can be one-dimensional.

Although they may not be present in the workplace, owners are still individuals and not faceless entities. They've made investments based on something they believe about your company. Learning what satisfies owners is a little difficult, especially when you have no direct contact with them, but it's not impossible. Your company's annual report might be a good place to start; it's written for shareholders and other individuals interested in the company's overall performance. You can also check the news. Look up articles about your company written by industry analysts or business journalists; you'll find information about how your company is performing in terms that are generally important to owners. One day, this information may prove useful in future interactions with your company's owners.

CONCLUSION: PEOPLE, PEOPLE, PEOPLE = TRUST, TRUST, TRUST

The word "trust" shows up quite a bit in this chapter. After all, trust is a key principle in the C.E.O. Satisfaction philosophy. Trust is very human and very personal. Leaders who establish and maintain trust with customers, employees, and owners—and all the sub-units within these three groups—consistently outperform their peers during both up and down market cycles. Creating and maintaining this trust is a complex challenge, but it is absolutely required to keep all stakeholders in alignment.

Successful leadership comes from the understanding that delivering an assignment is an opportunity to develop alignment. It's easy to deliver an assignment; managers do it all the time when delegating responsibility. But if you neglect to develop alignment, you miss out on an opportunity to build value for yourself as an effective leader. Developing alignment means simultaneously paying attention to your customers' needs, reinforcing employee satisfaction, and earning the trust of the business's owners. These are all examples of the strategic agility effective leaders develop throughout their careers: They practice experiential learning for themselves by finding people in their immediate sphere of influence who represent the key C.E.O. stakeholder groups, understanding their needs as people, and then satisfying them. The consequences of these decisions can be more significant later on, but the lessons themselves can be just as effective in leading to successful outcomes whenever they are learned.

I have one final thought to help solidify this foundational principle. When I needed to make a significant decision during my career, I used a test that I'll reference frequently. I call it "putting a face on it." I envisioned specific people in my customer, employee, and owner spheres and got comfortable that I could honestly articulate how this decision would affect them, positively and negatively, and why it was the right direction for the enterprise. Talking directly and honestly to a person who you want to remain committed and engaged in your business requires an understanding of his or her needs. If you can do that, it's a good decision.

CHAPTER 4

Defining Satisfaction for Customers

This is the first of three chapters in which we'll take an in-depth look at what satisfaction means for each of our three key stakeholder groups. These chapters are not intended to be complete and thorough reviews of satisfaction assessments. Instead, the focus here is on how to use C.E.O. Satisfaction to interpret assessment findings. The thing about research is that it usually generates more questions than answers, and therefore, it needs to be filtered through a C.E.O. Satisfaction lens. Without a set of grounding values, it's very easy to allow satisfaction research findings to lead you to a set of solutions that sound great generically but miss the mark for your specific key stakeholders. This is why developing a personal understanding of your stakeholders and maintaining alignment between them is so critical. They create your grounding values.

Let's begin with customers, which is a larger group than you might think. First of all, the simple definition of a customer is someone who has purchased, or will potentially purchase, a business's products or services. Customers are what actually makes a business viable. Without customers, a business will not generate revenue. Customers, then, are the most critical of the three stakeholder groups, because without customers, there's no way to satisfy employees or owners. Without customers, it's not a business. It's a hobby.

Within the umbrella term "customer," there are many different groups. There are direct purchasers, distribution partners (those who buy products from a company and sell them to others), and marketing partners (companies that merge elements of their businesses with elements of other businesses). A successful company satisfies the needs of these related, but very independent, types of purchasers.

The first step is to determine what will satisfy each of them. There are formal and informal techniques that can be used to do this, beginning with customer research. This is usually a formal process that involves surveys, analyses of customer purchase history, focus groups, competitive strategy analyses, and so on. Customer research is extremely valuable when properly designed and implemented. I've used several different techniques during my career, and I often found the research to be informative. In some cases, it became a catalyst for creative and strategic thinking. But I've also seen research findings be misinterpreted, with management teams hearing only what they wanted to hear. This is not uncommon. Management teams often look for answers that validate previous strategies or suggest strategies that can be easily implemented. The resulting decisions, therefore, often do not resonate with the customer base and knock stakeholder alignment out of whack. Here are a few examples for you to consider.

CAUTION! AUTOMATED TELEPHONE RESPONSE SYSTEMS AHEAD

Automated telephone response systems—the ones that ask us to "press '1' for new purchases" and "press '2' for existing orders"—are everywhere. They've become standard in many industries over the past ten to fifteen years, and they're now being supplanted by web-based self-service tools. Some of these web-based tools drive customer satisfaction, but many are not much better than the automated telephone systems.

In an effort to improve efficiency, which can be categorized as profitability, a major "satisfier" for owners, companies justify automated phone and web-based service models as "meeting" customer needs. Many of the service functions on these tools are quick and efficient: for example, access to basic information like mailing addresses, phone numbers, hours of operation, and account balances. But the design forces a self-serve model on all customers: every person has to listen to a menu of options or hunt around a web site in hopes of finding the route to their unique needs. If a caller or visitor doesn't understand the jargon or has a slightly more complex need, he or she is still forced to bounce through predesigned algorithms instead accessing a human who can help figure out a solution. When automated systems are used for things beyond basic information sharing and when they don't give customers the option to talk to a human being, automated response systems can be an example of losing balance and alignment; specifically, efficiency (owner satisfaction) is gained at the expense of personalized attention (customer satisfaction).

Customer research is used to determine which options to include in an automated telephone system's menu. These options might very well hit the mark most of the time, but it's impossible for them to address every customer's unique needs every time. Furthermore, it's easy enough to have a caller press "1" for new sale inquiries and "2" for inquiries about existing orders, for example, but things get complicated when cost-saving technology goes too far and companies design sub-menus and sub-sub-menus for their automated telephone systems. And callers aren't always given the option to press "0" for operator.

Another issue is the extent to which companies rely on automated telephone systems in the first place. Every time a customer is asked to make a selection using a keypad instead of talking to a human being, the company takes the risk of dissatisfying that customer. While some may argue that Americans are increasingly okay with systems that don't require talking to a live representative, there is still a sizable number of people who aren't. Is the money saved by using automated systems—instead of a call center staffed by human beings—worth alienating new or existing customers? Data might prove that automated systems get customers the right answer more quickly than call center representatives do, but is this something the customers themselves understand? What effects does an automated telephone system have on a company's brand image, particularly if that image is built on service and user friendliness?

All of this is not to argue that technology such as automated telephone systems should not be part of a company's customer service system. There are times when automated systems can be helpful, particularly if the system clearly routes callers efficiently. But how many times have you been frustrated with a company's telephone- or web-based self-service model? If you don't like the experience, why would your customers? Automated systems are great when they're used to look up basic information quickly, but customers often become frustrated when they run through a telephonic transfer tree two or three times or find themselves spending several minutes searching a web site for information. What's worse is when, while on hold, customers are forced to listen to a recorded message explaining the virtues of visiting a web site to solve their problems. This sends the awful message that the company really doesn't have time for its customers and would rather not spend the money that would allow a representative to talk to them.

My point here is not to rant and complain about self-service models. It's more about the decisions involved in designing and implementing them and how companies assess their success—and, of course, how their use might be approached by a C.E.O. Satisfaction practitioner. Like I mentioned earlier, put a face on the customer. Before convincing yourself that millennials and busy moms prefer a certain tool, such as an automated telephone system, consider an individual customer. Envision a millennial or a busy mom you know. Now envision them using the proposed tool. Are they satisfied with the experience? Are their interactions with the tool strengthening your brand? Is this tool maintaining stakeholder alignment? Along with formal research, envisioning your customers this way will help you develop a strategy that satisfies both your customers and your owners, optimizes operational savings, and improves customer satisfaction. Of course, the result might produce less operational savings than a more aggressive model would, but by engendering brand loyalty, your long-term return will be significantly better.

RENTING A CAR: SERVICING OR SUFFERING

In an effort to control travel costs, many businesses set up contracts with service providers such as car rental companies. My company had such a contract with a well-known car rental business, and we required traveling employees to use their services. This company used a customer service approach that involved personal attention from an individual representative throughout the many stages of the rental process. The representative would greet me at the airport, walk me to the car, describe the vehicle to me in detail, and then accompany me back to the counter to fill out the paperwork. This individual attention sounds great, and when successfully executed, it might be a powerful reason for customers to return to the business. I'm sure the company considered lots of customer satisfaction research data when developing this strategy. However, there were a few misalignment issues with it. When there were more customers than company representatives—due to several planes landing at the same time—people had to wait a long time to even begin the rental process. And once a representative was free, he or she would still walk through a very deliberate introduction to the car. This delay poses a problem with one of the most important expectations car rental customers have: getting on the road as quickly as possible. The extra personal touch this rental car company designed became more of an aggravation than anything else. Our employees eventually found ways to work around our requirement of using this particular car rental business, and we, in turn, changed to a more efficient provider.

Had the rental car company envisioned its customers while designing its customer service model, I'm sure they would have understood that their approach would not increase customer satisfaction and loyalty. Casual vacation travelers who do not rent cars often may appreciate the attention, but if casual travelers were the company's target customers, it should not have been chasing national agreements with businesses.

From a customer service perspective, the car rental company's strategy to "over deliver" backfired. This makes it a good example of how being out of alignment impacts other stakeholders. Let's look at employee satisfaction. At first glance, this customer service model might seem like a great opportunity for employees to interact with customers in more rewarding ways. They get to demonstrate their knowledge, answer questions, and feel like they made a difference. All good things. But what happens when the queue of customers waiting grows? The employees will begin to encounter an increasing number of impatient and grumpy customers, resulting in just the opposite experience. They can feel overwhelmed and personally responsible for the customers' irritation, which can ultimately reduce the employees' job satisfaction. Unsurprisingly, the car rental company in question no longer uses this customer service model.

DELIVERING ON YOUR PROMISES AND EXCEEDING EXPECTATIONS

Teams that develop business strategies sometimes forget that their customers have certain expectations about the goods or services the company offers. Successful companies maintain a crystal-clear understanding of these expectations and stay focused on meeting or exceeding them as much as possible. In fact, one of the most powerful ways a company can differentiate itself from the competition is effectively managing the times when its goods and services miss the mark.

No one bats a thousand, and businesses are no exception. When a company does come up short, its brand value and degree of customer satisfaction can be increased dramatically if the company addresses the resulting problems in a manner that demonstrates the company really cares about its customers and their expectations. As we discussed earlier in this chapter, and throughout this book, there are multiple ways to succeed in addressing most business challenges. Consistent with our earlier discussions, these actions are not "either or" choices. They are "both and."

A successful company makes sure to do them all. When it comes to addressing customer problems resulting from a company's mistakes or shortcomings, the first and obvious answer is to correct the problem itself. Replace a defective product, or provide additional services required to satisfy an unhappy customer. Unfortunately, it's easy to identify total industries that are not perceived as delivering on promises—cable companies, telephone companies, airlines, big banks, etc. Conversely, companies that deliver consistently and correct errors quickly are rewarded with loyalty. Nordstrom built its brand on service, Amazon is mastering online retail, Starbucks customizes your order, etc. Showing that a company "really" cares also involves the way customer service representatives convey empathy and demonstrate autonomy in solving customer problems.

Remember: do your research and then put a face on it.

A CHECKLIST TO DETERMINE IF YOUR COMPANY IS COMMITTED TO CUSTOMER SATISFACTION

Here is a simple test to help determine whether your company is achieving customer satisfaction. If any of the following statements have been made by your company's employees or managers, your focus on understanding and satisfying customer needs is almost surely compromised:

- "Our product works; it's just that our customers don't know how to use it."
- "We can [fill in the blank] to reduce product benefits and save production costs, and our customers won't ever notice it."

- "Our customers only want [fill in the blank with a specific product or service feature], and we don't need to give them anything more."

- "It only takes forty-five seconds to work through our automated telephone response system, and surveys show customers don't get frustrated until sixty seconds have passed, so we're okay."

- "Older people don't know how to use technology, and younger people don't want to talk with live people on the telephone. As our customers age out, our reliance on technology will develop into a good business decision."

- "If we cut costs, our survey shows that we'll continue to satisfy ninety percent of our customers; we can afford to risk the ten percent we might lose in the process."

On the other hand, if you hear statements like the ones listed below, chances are you're working in an organization that's making good efforts to learn how to meet the needs of its customers:

- "We have a high probability of building a loyal customer base if we focus on the four things that make our service valuable to them and measure performance on those things every day."

- "There are processes in place to quickly and urgently correct any reported failures."

- "We can create systems to monitor our reported failures, our competitors' marketplace moves, and our regular communication with our customers, and we can use this information to constantly review and refine our business practices to minimize harm and maximize benefits in these areas."

- "No one on our team should ever downplay or disrespect the decision-making ability of our customer base."

CHAPTER 5

Defining Satisfaction for Employees

Our second key stakeholder group is a business's employees. As with customers, the intent here is not to provide an exhaustive review of satisfaction analytics and solutions. Instead, we'll discuss how to use C.E.O Satisfaction to identify and implement the most effective (and most aligned) solutions. Employee satisfaction can be fairly difficult to maintain, especially if your company is large enough to have several functional units and multiple layers of management.

Let's begin this chapter with a look at things we can do to keep our employees satisfied. In order to become the successful leader the C.E.O. Satisfaction approach promises, it's important to understand who your employees are and what might motivate and de-motivate them to achieve the company's strategic goals.

"One size does not fit all" is an important adage when considering employee satisfaction and engagement. In fact, a strategy for satisfying employees is actually a collection of several strategies, each aimed at a particular subset of this stakeholder group. Great leaders, particularly those who practice C.E.O. Satisfaction, not only take the time to understand the different drivers behind employee satisfaction, but they also adjust and adapt their own behaviors to reinforce those drivers.

Companies that are regularly voted the best places to work understand that the key to satisfying employees is engaging them. Engaged employees have four characteristics:

- They understand what's best for the entire company and can see the path corporate leaders have created to get there.

- They believe they can make important individual and team contributions to the organization's success.

- The contributions they make are recognized and rewarded.

- They have the opportunity to grow and develop within the company.

To create a workforce with these values and this sense of commitment, a leader must accept the responsibility for articulating the company's mission in a way employees can understand. The leader must also convince employees that the work they do makes a real difference, because the leader honestly believes this is true. It's the only way to make sure employees are appreciated and respected for the contributions they make. The only way a leader can effectively do all of these things is by understanding and knowing the company's employees. In other words, leaders have to "put a face" to their audience to test the effectiveness of their messages and strategies.

C.E.O Satisfaction

Hopefully you've worked for leaders who were able to establish employee engagement. In my career, I've witnessed the good, the bad, and the ugly of leadership. Much of my approach to C.E.O. leadership was formed from these experiences. My first job out of college was at a company with a great employee satisfaction culture. Senior executives routinely and spontaneously joined lower-level employees at their cafeteria lunch tables. These interactions were not scripted or oriented toward company infomercials. They were simple social exchanges in which the executives freely answered questions about themselves and asked how the employees were doing. Most of the lower-level employees felt that these exchanges were sincere efforts to understand the needs of employees. Consequently, we trusted that the executives considered our needs when making decisions. Later in my career, I took a second-in-command role to a CEO who was the poster child for MBWA (management by walking around). He knew every employee's name and much of their background. He made a daily habit of circulating through the operations floor to say hello or thank you and was always available for direct conversation if requested. As a result, his employees completely trusted him.

On the flip side, I've also seen the bad and the ugly. In one case, the entire executive team positioned themselves on the fiftieth floor of a nearby building and never ventured elsewhere. The only way to interact with them was if you happened to be summoned for a meeting. Of course, these meetings usually felt more like critiques than anything else. You can imagine that not many people were anxious to get an invitation. Another CEO was put in place by the owners and tasked with "fixing things." He had no interest in the existing culture, the employees' perspectives, or even the customers. He was only interested in showing the owners that he could improve profitability, which, obviously, did not help the business move forward. In both cases, any attempt by the leadership to communicate directions to employees was met with significant skepticism.

Of course, you'll want to be remembered as one of the good leaders—not the bad, and certainly not the ugly. Later on in this chapter, I'll help you build the skills necessary to be a good leader.

PARTIES, PIZZA, AND PING PONG: CAUTION!

Over the past ten to fifteen years, primarily due to millennials entering the workforce and tech startups popping up everywhere, leaders have begun perceiving fun activities in the workplace as drivers of employee engagement. I'll admit that I can't pass a shuffleboard table or dart board without taking a few tries, but I think their presence in the workplace can frequently be extraneous. I strongly believe that without a strong, sustained commitment to the four foundational characteristics of employee engagement, fun activities are nothing more than window dressing. I think this is true for millennials and baby boomers, high school graduates and college graduates, female employees and male employees, front-line workers and senior executives—basically everybody. Again, the four characteristics of engaged employees are as follows:

- Understanding what the company is trying to achieve.
- Being confident that their contributions matter.
- Receiving recognition for their contributions
- Having the opportunity to learn and develop skills for future roles.

Unless employees have these foundational characteristics in place, no amount of fun parties, perks, or morale campaigns can create real engagement. Fun activities may lead to short-term spikes in productivity or on-the-job satisfaction, but a dependence on these sorts of motivational programs almost certainly will not last. However, once the four foundational characteristics have been well established, then other perks or policies could be beneficial—and even crucial—to your workforce. Flexibility in work hours, parental leave, excellent medical and disability plans, and creative bonuses are all great ways to attract and retain talent. They just need to be layered on top of a solid foundation. Let me share an anecdote from my own experience.

I had just joined a midsized company that was at a critical time in its evolution. It had enjoyed tremendous growth and was at the point of changing from a small, "everyone knows your name" environment to one with more structure and complexity. Employees who were used to the good old days were struggling with these changes, and overall satisfaction was diminishing. Around that time, we hired a new human resources director with lots of experience and enthusiasm. The CEO commissioned a satisfaction survey of employees, and the results were disappointing. He directed the new HR head to implement solutions aimed at improving employee morale and engagement. Over the next few years, the HR director implemented two separate programs that improved employee morale but actually hurt the company as a whole.

The first program involved fun activities like in the good old days: contests, celebrations, perks, external career coaches, and so on. There was an activity nearly every week: a special luncheon, a Friday karaoke contest, and even a monthly massage day (he brought a team of masseuses in for this). Many people enjoyed these perks, but the problem was that they were not at all connected to the company's performance. Whether we were doing well or poorly, we were always celebrating. These activities became more of an entitlement rather than an aligned reward for good performance. Consequently, it became difficult for our operational managers to support these programs while also delivering great results. Our employees were happier, but they were not really engaged, and our customers and owners were not seeing any of the benefits. It took us a while to realize the mistake, since the initiative did immediately improve employee morale. The problem was compounded by the second program, which was implemented at the same time and had a similar short-term success followed by long-term problems.

This second program provided a new way to handle employee relations. Due to the company's rapid growth, many front line and middle managers were promoted from within, and were not necessarily skilled in employee relations. This contributed to employees not feeling supported or respected by the company. The HR director's solution was to take direct control of all employee relations, thus removing an important responsibility from the managers. This created a number of problems as this program developed. While the company did see short-term improvement in employee relations, managers stopped receiving the training necessary to handle these issues on their own. Later on, another, more serious problem developed. Over time, the human resources staff became the "white knights" in the eyes of the employees, while the managers were the goats. Instead of aligning and strengthening relations between managers and their employees, the HR director's system created rifts.

There was a host of other problems, as well: employees lost

their sense of alignment with the company mission and with their management teams; money that could have been used to add staff or train managers was spent on fun activities and on the expansion of the human resources department; and, worst of all, the goal of fostering happy employees began to supersede the goals of satisfying customers and owners. Needless to say, changes were made and a balanced model was restored, but the company experienced significant disruptions and was forced to reset employee expectations. The entire experience turned out to be a classic example of swinging the pendulum too far and creating new problems while trying to solve the one at hand.

WHO IS AN EMPLOYEE?

This may seem like a silly question, but it's one that needs to be discussed. Employees are the people on a company's payroll. However, there are several other groups that play key roles in delivering a product or service to customers. Consider the growing use of independent contractors, such as the ones used by Uber and Airbnb. Also consider critical suppliers and outsourced customer service representatives. While these people are not employees in the absolute sense, they're very similar to employees in a practical sense. Therefore, it's important to apply the C.E.O. Satisfaction approach to these groups as well. The goal here is the same: in order to engage them, they need a sense of direction, a sense of purpose, and a sense of value—though the strategies you employ here may be a bit different from the ones you use for traditional employees. Designing strategies for "win/win" partnerships, however, helps ensure that your customers' expectations are met.

THE ALL-IMPORTANT RELATIONSHIP BETWEEN EMPLOYEES AND THEIR WORK ENVIRONMENT

Learning how to satisfy employees versus learning how to satisfy customers and owners is a little easier and a little more complex. Although you may be a customer of your company's services and may have a small ownership stake, your biggest role is as an employee. You operate every day within the work environment along with all of the other employees. As a NEO, you have a terrific opportunity to hone your C.E.O. Satisfaction skills and understand how they relate to employees. This is the best time and place for learning the skills that are so essential to engaging employees as a senior leader; it's a time to look at what these skills are and how to teach them to yourself during the early stages of your career—a "curriculum" for this training program, if you will.

Remember, when you talk to employees (your coworkers and direct reports), make sure to never take part in negative chatter or gossip. This doesn't mean ignoring these conversations; by all means, learn from them and listen to employee complaints. This will allow you to gain valuable information about the roots of their concerns, which will be important later on in your career. Be sure, however, to separate yourself from "factions" engaged in these conversations. Do not become part of the dissatisfied group, and be comfortable in knowing that you don't have to try and change anyone's opinion. Your main role in these conversations is to engage in them honestly and figure out the cause of your fellow employees' dissatisfaction.

You'll learn that the roots of satisfaction and dissatisfaction generally come down to one or more of the following "workplace factors."

1. Communication

Do the employees know what's going on? Have the employees interpreted what's going on correctly?

> The positive: Knowing what's going on and believing that the company is doing the right thing makes employees confident and even excited.

> The negative: When employees sense that information is being withheld from them, they can feel disrespected and underappreciated. They may even feel that the company's leaders are out of touch with not only their employees, but also with customers, other stakeholder groups, and the industry as a whole.

2. Work Effectiveness

Does the organizational structure support employees' ability to achieve their individual and collective goals? Do employees feel that there are built-in barriers to getting the job done?

> The positive: The belief that the organization is structured to support the achievement of one's (or one's team's) goals results in a feeling of optimism that it is possible or even likely that work goals can be accomplished.

> The negative: A belief that there are inherent barriers to personal or team success can result in a pessimistic or even defeatist mentality.

3. Personal Value

Do the bosses know what I do and do they appreciate my contributions? Is the company's reward system fair, and are the rules for rewards and recognition well understood? Are there ample opportunities for professional growth?

> The positive: The answers to these questions can create a strong sense of commitment and teamwork.

> The negative: The answers can also create an equally strong sense of apathy or even resistance to managerial initiatives. Of course, there is always the possibility that an employee's feelings of being undervalued or mismanaged are not accurate. If that is the case, the option of trying to intervene and correct this misunderstanding must be weighed against the option of limiting damage by isolating the individual from others. This is a dilemma every leader must learn to deal with. And, as is often the case, it's best to learn how to deal with these situations early on in your career.

While I believe these three workplace factors encompass most sources of satisfaction and dissatisfaction in the workplace, I don't want to restrict you from adding to the list. As you assess your company and employees, feel free to expand it. As I mentioned in Chapter 3, the key to almost all managerial successes and failures comes down to the same three things: "People, people, people."

Understanding workplace factors like communication, work effectiveness, and personal value is an important first step. Learning what to do about these factors requires an additional step, which involves looking at your coworkers and employees as individuals, independent of their workplace roles, and identifying their unique characteristics. In other words, put a face on it. Combining these two perspectives—workplace factors and individual characteristics—is the key to developing a repertoire of motivational strategies for your employees. Specifically, once a leader has mastered the ability of using workplace factors to assess morale, he or she can then assess the employees' individual qualities to create a solid plan for maintaining employee satisfaction. Because leaders of large organizations must delegate these tasks to others, it is vital that they develop these skills in the early stages of their careers, when it's possible to interact with individual employees on a personal level. The key to success with people, people, people is to practice, practice, practice.

A successful leader recognizes the different needs of employees as individuals and as a member of a group. You can practice assessing employee satisfaction by first recognizing some of the general categories employees typically fall into, which have been listed below. For some, this is a permanent state, but for most, the category depends on the person's job and the workplace environment. Here are my thoughts on ways to group employees into categories based on their individual characteristics.

A. The solid citizen

A solid citizen is a good worker who has a positive attitude but who views a job as the means to an end. For solid citizens, this end is almost never work related. The end could be providing for the worker's family or financing personal interests and hobbies. To keep solid citizens engaged, a manager will need to provide them with the tools to do their job well; offer them fair pay; maintain a workplace environment that fosters good employee relationships; and, perhaps most importantly, allow them to leave their work at the office at the end of each day.

B. The underutilized

These are basically solid citizens with untapped potential. They don't expect anything more than solid citizens do, as they also assume they are mere worker bees. However, these individuals have talent and, if prodded, will take on additional challenges. They'll need encouragement and a safety net to make them feel more confident, but once they see what they're capable of, these workers can develop into strong middle managers, or maybe even senior corporate staffers. They become incredibly engaged once they're able to see their full potential, and they're highly appreciative of being given the opportunity to do so. In addition to being a cheerleader and providing a safety net, the key to managing workers in this category is to be skilled at identifying their potential and to provide support for the development of skills tailored to their individual needs.

C. The grinder

These are the people who are always overloaded with work; they frequently complain about how much they need to get done, but in fact they're working hard because they want to. They believe that they can handle the work that no one else wants to do (maybe even the work that no one else *can* do) and that this is their value within the organization. Grinders appreciate being recognized for their unique contributions, and to satisfy them, managers should continually assign them "tough" jobs—although they'll never actually seem satisfied.

D. The specialist

These employees want to be the best at something. They want to believe they are the unique go-to people. They are often department experts, but they may also be the most knowledgeable people in the company about an obscure legacy process or product. Their satisfaction comes from being recognized for their unique expertise. In many cases, this satisfaction is self-sustaining; like grinders, specialists enjoy being asked to provide their services and may be happiest when they believe they are solving a crisis. The difference for specialists is the fact that their identity is strongly linked to their unique skill set. Therefore, managers can increase specialists' satisfaction by providing them training to hone their skills. It also doesn't hurt to recognize their importance in both formal and informal ways.

E. The leader

Many people begin their careers by wanting to climb the ladder to the top. However, in my experience, this changes quickly with time. The number of people in the workforce who are truly willing to make the investments required to be an organizational leader is surprisingly small. The benefits are attractive—power, money, title, recognition—but true leaders are driven more by the success of the enterprise than by personal rewards. They are willing to shoulder their share of the responsibility for overall success and will gladly put their personal interests behind those of the organization. If you're reading this book, you're probably one of these people. You're motivated by challenge and the promise of increased responsibility.

The risk in managing leaders is that they're very sensitive to the possibility of opportunities passing them by. When that happens, dissatisfaction creeps in. This is the tricky part of managing leaders: they should be challenged and encouraged, but only up to a point. Not everyone becomes a CEO, so most people hit a wall somewhere, and when they do, they'll need to face the realization that they've stopped ascending the corporate ladder. This is the most difficult point in time for these individuals—and for their managers. These employees can continue to provide valuable contributions and may even become solid citizens; conversely, if they feel they have been the victims of poor communication, an unfair work environment, or an incorrect assessment of their personal value, they can become bad apples (see below).

F. The incapable

Sometimes the wrong people are hired for the job. Other times, job requirements shift dramatically and employees can't keep up. It's unfortunate, but it's that simple. There are individuals who are well intentioned and work hard but simply do not have the skill set necessary for success. Sadly, they are most likely destined for repeated failures, and eventually dissatisfaction will set in. Removing an incapable employee is the quickest remedy, but there is a better option: providing honest feedback about their performance, followed by efforts to offer training or support to help them succeed. If after a few attempts there's no improvement, they should be counseled to move on to a new workplace. It's important to make sure the entire process is handled in a fair and caring manner. If the employee needs to leave the organization, the other employees should be able to clearly understand and appreciate the managerial efforts that were taken. Winning and maintaining their trust depends on it.

G. The bad apple

Unhappy and constantly dissatisfied, this type of employee disagrees with the company, dislikes most of the bosses, and would rather not be working there, or perhaps anywhere, at all. We all know the type. They deserve one quick opportunity to adjust, and if it fails, they should be removed. Remember that managers have a responsibility to their teams; they can't jeopardize the success of the group by paying too much attention to one bad apple. There is no need for managers to be vindictive, although they will need to act decisively and relatively quickly if it's clear that efforts to provide training or support are being rebuffed. There is a clear difference between bad apples and incapable individuals, and it's not just managers who know the type—everyone else does, too.

R.E.S.P.E.C.T.: THAT'S WHAT IT MEANS

Unless you are the child of a lifelong CEO and every member of your family and your circle of friends are CEOs, then you have witnessed the impact of work life on individuals, well before you started your own career. And it's likely that over those years you heard of great stories and horrible ones. The good ones have a common theme that the horror stories don't: The good ones involve being "aligned" with the company (or boss), being "valued" by the company (or boss), and being respected by the company (or boss).

Successful leaders ensure that all employees are treated with respect. They understand that the company values its employees and their contributions. Ensuring respect is perhaps the single most important responsibility of a successful leader. Respect is an intangible commodity, and it must be expressed in a number of ways for employees to recognize it. It begins with interactions between employees and direct supervisors. Therefore, managers, other corporate staff members, and even employees themselves need to be taught how and why to treat every employee with respect. This company-wide commitment to mutual respect and appreciation starts at the top, and it doesn't start on the day someone becomes the CEO. It starts well before that, in the earliest days of our careers.

The C.E.O. Satisfaction model doesn't provide answers to every issue; it provides a value system and a focus on alignment. Throughout your career, you'll likely have to make many decisions that do not benefit all employees; I'm not suggesting dodging these tough situations. But by practicing assessing, aligning, and achieving satisfaction, you'll develop the trust and respect necessary to implement difficult decisions without disrupting the business.

WHO CAN TEACH A LEADER HOW TO ENGAGE EMPLOYEES?

So far in this chapter, I've discussed ways a manager or senior leader can achieve employee satisfaction. How does someone who is not yet in a position to have access to the results of human resources reports, surveys, and white papers practice these skills? What can NEOs do to ensure that their workplace interactions yield valuable insights? How does someone learn to explain the organization's mission clearly and in a way that motivates employees? Where do NEOs acquire the interpersonal skills needed to ensure all employees feel appreciated and respected? Finally, who teaches NEOs how to build a strong foundation of trust?

My answer is simple, if unsurprising. The teacher is the NEO, and the training grounds are the various positions the NEO holds in the workplace. Not to beat a dead horse (or in this case, an old customer service department in Cincinnati), but by the time I learned many of these skills, I was running a small operation within my company. My ability to communicate with my employees about how we were doing taught me how to be successful. Practicing teamwork and developing strong interpersonal skills are invaluable for a successful leader, and early on in your career, you can make and correct communication mistakes relatively easily. Also, your creative ideas can become reality more easily, as you may not need the formal proposals, reviews, and documentation that may be required at the highest levels of a large corporation.

In fact, it's essential for an NEO working in the lower rungs of the corporate ladder to develop C.E.O skills before moving upwards. It's only at these lower levels that fellow employees will view the NEO with a "one of us" mentality, which will allow the employees to be more honest and open in sharing ideas, thoughts, and even criticisms with the NEO. A senior leader, even one who frequently engages with employees, most likely will not receive the same open, honest feedback from lower-level employees. A senior leader is more likely to be seen as "one of them," and employees will instinctively try to manage their interactions with him or her, making a direct exchange of honest and valuable information more difficult to achieve.

A TEST TO DETERMINE HOW SATISFIED YOUR COWORKERS ARE

I'll close this chapter with two informal assessment tools you can use to gain insights into (1) how satisfied your coworkers are and (2) what types of employees exist in your sphere of influence. Please note that these tests are not scientific; they are intended for personal use only.

The main purpose of the first test is to turn the concepts discussed in this chapter into elements of a satisfaction assessment tool.

Begin with the vertical axis of this grid. From top to bottom, list (1) "fair pay and benefits," (2) "clear understanding of company goals and individual role in them," (3) "effective training and appropriate tools/environment to meet objectives," and (4) "treated with respect." Along the horizontal axis at the top of the grid, list (A) "me," (B) "my employees," and (C) "my peers." In each box listed under "People," write "yes" if the things listed in the corresponding "Workplace Factors" box satisfies this group and "no" if they do not. Use your managerial sense, and remember the things you've seen and heard on the job. A very informal gut feel is fine for the purposes of this exercise. Once you've completed the chart, take a look at your "yes" and "no" answers. What can you learn from them? Do all constituents feel good about the workplace factors in play? If they do, that's terrific; if not, spend some time thinking about who doesn't feel good, and why. How would you make them feel more engaged?

	People		
Workplace Factors	Me	My employees	My peers
Fair pay and benefits			
Clear understanding of company goals and individual role in them			
Effective training and appropriate tools/ environment to meet objectives			
Treated with respect			

Figure 1

For the second assessment tool, pick a half dozen of your direct reports or peers and determine which category best describes them, using the list provided earlier in this chapter (solid citizen, grinder, leader, etc.). Is the organization employing appropriate satisfaction and engagement strategies for these people? If not, what would you do differently? Now put yourself in the category that you think your senior leaders would use to describe you. Is this where you want to be? If your answer is yes, are you receiving the reinforcement and satisfaction you need? If not, which category would you like to be in? What will you need to do in order to change your managers' and bosses' perceptions of you?

I hope these exercises help you convert some of my more conceptual ideas about employee satisfaction into more tangible assessments. Even if you are not yet in the position to take any managerial action based these findings, the important takeaway is your ability to define and assess real, personal satisfaction for yourself, your employees, and your peers. If you can learn to assess and manage satisfaction correctly on a small scale, you can do it on a large scale, too. Eventually, these assessment and managerial skills will work for you when you become a senior manager, or even a CEO.

Most employee satisfaction evaluation tools are solid and useful, but to use them, you'll need a strong, internalized strategic framework to base your interpretations and actions on. The C.E.O approach will enable you to differentiate faddish or academic proposals from real, effective, sustainable solutions. As is the case with any type of business expertise, trends in employee management will come and go. But your C.E.O. managerial philosophy will enable you to maintain a focus on using your assessment skills and managerial tools to define, reach, and maintain a balance of satisfaction among your employees—and also among all three key constituent groups.

CHAPTER 6

Defining Satisfaction for Owners

Next we'll focus on owners. As with the previous two chapters, I'll begin with a definition. On the surface, this seems relatively easy. Owners are the individuals and organizations who have invested money or time ("sweat equity") in a company—and they expect financial returns on their investments. There are a few types of owners, and all of them are a bit different. These differences are based on the individual owner's reason to invest. As it turns out, there are only a few basic reasons to invest in a company; therefore, there are only a few types of owners. Knowing a company's investors and their reasons for investing will help leadership understand what drives their satisfaction and how to maintain it. Maintaining the emphasis on the human beings who compose each of our key stakeholder groups, you'll notice that my discussion of owners begins with the reasons behind their investments. (Please note that the terms "investor" and "owner" are interchangeable here.)

REASONS FOR INVESTING IN A COMPANY

There are three basic reasons people invest in companies. There are many sophisticated variations, but at the core, the reasons are change in share value, cash generation, or a hunch.

1. Shares increase in value over some targeted timeline and can be sold

Investments based on this logic are made under the assumption that the company will increase in value at a rate exceeding that of the market. These investors believe they see a competitive advantage in the company (based on such fundamentals as unique products or services, outstanding management, and opportunities resulting from synergies if or when the company merges with other companies), or there is potential to re-engineer or restructure the company. These investors are primarily motivated by the opportunity to buy lower and sell higher and may not have a deep interest in the inner workings of the company beyond its ability to generate a strong return on their investment.

2. Dividends

Investors motivated by dividends believe a company has a track record of generating cash and distributing it to shareholders. These investors may not be overly concerned about whether the value of the company increases; they are more concerned with its ability to create steady annual returns through regular and reliable dividend payments.

3. Belief

These types of investors ultimately evolve into one of the first two types, but their underlying driver is their belief that either the company's products or its management team (or both) are worth the bet. Believers can be great allies or a management team's worst nightmare, depending on the amount of influence they have (e.g., their ownership stake) and their ability to respect their roles as "governors" of the organization and not the day-to-day managers. Believers can also include employees who purchase stock through the company's benefits plan. They can be the best owners of all because they believe in their own abilities and the abilities of their colleagues to create value.

Ideally, a company will have a mix of investors representing each of these categories. A successful leader will be skilled at making the case that the company will generate a strong financial return and that investors ought to have faith in its future. In most cases, however, the pool of investors will likely be dominated by one of these categories. It's important to get to know a company's owners in order to effectively satisfy them.

CHALLENGES FOR COMPANY LEADERS: THE OWNERS ARE WATCHING

No matter which category best describes your company's investors, they are an important stakeholder group. Collectively, they hold ultimate decision-making power over all issues, including the employment of the CEO and his or her management team. They're always watching the company, as they may need to intervene in order to improve performance. Even though most NEOs won't have direct contact with owners until later in their careers, thinking about them as individual people can help you understand who they are and how they're likely to behave. Furthermore, knowing what satisfies your company's owners will help you make sure your actions are aligned with the organization's overarching goals.

Here are a few examples from my experience—some from the early days of my career—that can help even the most junior NEO understand the challenges of satisfying owners.

Challenge One: Revenue is not always predictable or guaranteed.

Customers and competitors don't always operate as anticipated. For example, predicting gross revenue is the starting point of any budget process, but predictions are frequently unreliable. Will the company be able to retain current sales figures when customers inevitably start changing their behaviors? Will strategies to draw in new purchasers have the intended effect during the timeframe and at the projected levels? Is the company able to manage pricing and distribution costs? Can the external strategy be adjusted if expected prices or overall sales levels change? More importantly, how can internal attitudes be adjusted in order to support the strategic changes brought about by unexpected developments?

Early in my career I attended a very enjoyable and effective marketing training program. There were about twenty-five of us in the program; all of us were business leaders or marketing professionals. The program used a virtual marketplace as a training tool. The marketplace included five competing companies, and participants were divided into five teams, each team representing a fictional company to run. At the start of the program, the teams received information about their companies, as well as some basic market data, and developed a strategy to grow the business using things like pricing, sales efforts, new product innovation, and so on. There were five cycles in the program; in each cycle, we received new data about changes in the marketplace. Our challenge, then, was to make adjustments based on these changes. At the end of each cycle, we submitted our adjusted strategies. The new strategies of each team were collected and then distributed to the other teams before the next cycle began. This provided each team with feedback on how the various strategies worked relative to one another. Did market share go up or down? Was profitability improved? How did the strategies of different companies affect the success or failure of the others?

After all five cycles, a winner was declared, as were the losers. The team that generated the least profitable growth was led by a highly respected and very successful marketing executive. When asked for feedback on the program, the executive was visibly upset and said the game wasn't accurate because his competitors didn't make good decisions or act rationally. How could he possibly succeed in an irrational marketplace? Obviously, he was not a good loser, and he was understandably embarrassed. But the real value of the program may have been lost on him. The main learning experience—at least, for me—was to see how dynamic a marketplace could truly be. It can be extremely challenging to plan and execute top-line performance.

Challenge Two: Market conditions

We can't always see the challenges coming around the corner, but the goal of a leader practicing the C.E.O. Satisfaction approach is to develop the radar to detect changes as early as possible, and to adapt as quickly as possible. How much is your business directly affected by macro market trends? What systems do you have in place for learning about these trends as they emerge? How quickly can leaders develop effective plans to react to these larger trends, minimize damage, and take advantage new opportunities?

We can look to the healthcare industry for an example of how larger trends effect a marketplace. For many medical providers, Medicare patients may make up between twenty and forty percent of their business. Medicare sets reimbursement rates annually, and it requires any provider that admits Medicare patients to accept Medicare reimbursements as full payments. In other words, providers cannot collect more than the Medicare payment for an individual patient. Medicare has struggled to control costs, and there have been some significant reductions in reimbursement rates as a result. These reductions are usually announced as part of Medicare's annual reimbursement levels; they come out in early November and are implemented on January 1, eight weeks later. As a result, many healthcare businesses learn that their Medicare reimbursements will drop ten to forty percent and have just eight weeks to plan accordingly. This poses a real challenge, especially considering that Medicare patients make up twenty to forty percent of a healthcare business.

Dealing with unexpected and uncontrollable changes in the market requires making the situation as expected and controllable as possible. Medicare reimbursements have been a problem in the medical field for years, and adapting to annual reductions is nothing new. Leaders in industries that are subject to external changes must be good communicators: their stakeholder groups need to be aware that theirs is an industry that can be dramatically affected—both positively and negatively—by outside forces. Leaders must also develop a broad framework for dealing with these changes. The first tactics used should be those with the least impact on long-term operations, with the subsequent tactics increasing in severity. All stakeholder groups will benefit from the knowledge that leadership is aware of the risks external forces pose on a company and has plans for dealing with them. Owners, however, are the ones most likely to expect changes and therefore may judge a company harshly if risk mitigation strategies are not in place.

Challenge Three: Talking yourself into a strategic direction.

Unlike the first two challenges, the next few describe self-inflicted wounds. These typically occur when a company's strategic plan is based on faulty logic. Sometimes this happens because strategy development is too process driven, and planners lose the ability to differentiate the forest from the trees—much like the marketing executive, who lost the management game described earlier in this chapter, did. A good leader knows when a company is headed toward self-inflicted wounds. Signs include situations in which real planning stalls while analysis continues, or when time seems to be running short in the planning schedule well before a clear strategy – or even the outline of one – is apparent to everyone on the team. These are the environments in which managers talk themselves into problematic strategies. Everyone knows a conclusion needs to be drawn, so leaders convince themselves that a strategic direction will be successful when it's likely the result of lowest common denominator thinking. This mistake almost always results in the significant loss of time, energy, and money, and the strategy will at best underperform and at worst fail miserably. A successful leader can see this mistake coming and will redirect the planning process. Extending the planning timeframe or even taking a break from planning in order to clear out the unfocused thinking that has gotten in the way is a far better solution than plodding ahead toward an artificial time deadline and implementing a poorly conceived strategy.

Challenge Four: Interpreting market data without gut-level understanding.

Managers must be careful to not misinterpret or even completely ignore data in favor of simply relying on gut feeling. Once again, balance is key. Here is an example of this challenge, also from the healthcare insurance industry. A few years ago, in an effort to improve the efficiency and effectiveness of its customer service and claims operations, a large health insurance company brought in a leader from one of its largest clients, a consumer banking company. The insurance company, which had become somewhat ineffective as it grew in size, suddenly felt an energy and urgency under the new management. There was a new emphasis on giving clients what they wanted, and employees became willing to embrace change. Fairly quickly, this new leader became president of the business.

Based on his experience as a former client, he was convinced that the company's customers wanted streamlined and standardized services and support. Confident that these improvements would lead the company to new levels of success, he embarked on a major infrastructure redesign to simplify operations, reduce costs, and market the benefits of these changes to the company's large clients. What he didn't fully understand was that seventy percent of his business came from clients who liked the company because of its flexibility, while only fifteen percent were primarily interested in low costs. He was a very smart man, and he knew the importance of checking data to verify his assumptions before acting. However, data was captured at this company in such a way that the revenue and profit contribution from large clients were distributed across several product lines, and the low-cost market was linked to a bundled product line, resulting in these clients appearing to be a much larger contributor than they were. Compounding the problem was the fact that several other members of his team were relatively new, and none of them picked up on the fact that the information they were receiving was based on a misaligned reporting. As a result, the company experienced several challenging years of poor sales and profitability, eventually resulting in a change of leadership. Not surprisingly, the board of directors decided to go back to industry veterans.

Challenge Five: Thinking that you're Steve Jobs

Steve Jobs had the ability to design what people wanted before people knew it themselves. And under his leadership, Apple brought products to market that changed the world and drove unprecedented growth. There are similar success stories in the internet-based economy, and as a result, some leaders think that they can and should be the sole providers of vision for their businesses. In their minds, the new profile of successful leaders includes the ability to decide what other people want. There are two problems with this approach. First, a strategy based on a single person being right in a way no one else can imagine cannot be adequately evaluated; it's an extremely high-risk adventure at best, and it goes against the checks and balances that are part of the C.E.O. Satisfaction approach. Second, Steve Jobs was one in a million. He lived at the perfect time for his skills and abilities, and Apple was the perfect place for him to put his skills to use. The odds that any other individual has the same skills and abilities and is in the perfect business at the perfect time are extremely low.

Before embarking on a quest to prove you're the next Steve Jobs, think about how you would react if one of your coworkers tried to convince you he or she was the next big thing. Equally important, how would your customers, employees, and owners react?

Challenge Six: Internal budget battles

It's practically a universal law of business that at any given time, there is significantly more demand for budget dollars than there is available money. Every department naturally thinks that its need is greater than the needs of others, so in most annual planning processes, the sum of the budget requests greatly exceeds a profitable financial plan. There are four possible outcomes of a budget planning process; three of them are bad, and only one is good. And all three of the poor ones result in misaligned allocation of available dollars. We'll start with the bad outcomes.

First, every department receives a budget that's less than what was asked for. As a result, no one has enough money to implement improvements. The company, then, nets a poor return for any increased dollars spent, since none of the proposed initiatives are funded well enough to be successful.

The second bad outcome results from approving everyone's increases and balancing the budget by building unreasonable top-line expectations for increased revenue. As I mentioned earlier, top-line projections are always very challenging. Internal spending, on the other hand, is usually fairly easy to predict. In this case, it's almost certain that projected income will fall short while spending will stay as predicted. The company, then, won't reach its target profits.

The third bad outcome is brought about by selectively approving the wrong budget increases. This can happen if there are so many requests that none of them can be evaluated carefully.

The one good outcome occurs when leaders only consider budget increases that clearly support the company's overall strategy. My best advice is to fund these requests and kill the others. Then, sequence these investments in order to maximize results and minimize profitability risk. Check that you've sequenced investments properly by creating timelines and checking actual progress against projected progress.

THREE QUESTIONS TO ANSWER IN SATISFYING OWNERS

As we wind down this chapter, let's take an honest look at the following question: what does my company need to do to satisfy the owners? Your company can develop an effective owner satisfaction program much like its employee satisfaction programs. Care must be taken while developing such a program, but that doesn't mean it can't or shouldn't be attempted. Start with an organizational assessment; you can use the following questions to complete this simple exercise.

- What do you know about the ownership? Define your company's primary investors. Who owns the majority of the company? Are they public or private investors? Are they institutional or individual investors? What is the makeup of your company's board of directors? How do your company's employees and senior managers participate in ownership?
- What are the pros and cons of investing in your company? What do Wall Street analysts says about your company? What does the industry press say about it? Read your annual report. How would you feel about the company if you relied on the annual report alone for information? What's left out? What questions do you have about the company after reviewing these materials? How would you improve things for current and future investors?

- How do external analyses of the company compare with the company's own strategic objectives? Do you believe that outside descriptions of the company's strategy match descriptions given by the owners and senior managers? If so, how does this position the company for future success? If not, how are these sources misaligned, and what can be done to realign them?

WHAT CAN YOU DO?

The final section of Chapter 6 is an exercise to help you assess your company's owner satisfaction program. How can you contribute to the following financial levers? Though you might not have direct responsibility for them, you can find ways to improve each of them. In each box under "People," list the respective ways you, your employees, and your peers can move the corresponding financial lever in a positive direction.

	People		
Financial levers	Me	My employees	My peers
Revenue: price, units, margin			
Scale: productivity and efficiency			
Cash flow			
Return on capital investment			

Figure 2

CHAPTER 7

Finding and Maintaining Balance

THE NEXT TWO chapters move away from the theory of C.E.O. Satisfaction to move into its use and practical application. This is where we shift the focus to you: are you prepared to distinguish yourself as leader? This chapter will focus on clarifying your self-image and self-management objectives. This is where you take charge of your goals and create your own roadmap in learning how to be a great leader.

The leader's role is not simply to manage. It is to orchestrate and organize, to align and balance, and to ensure that the wide variety of stakeholder interests are identified, managed, and effectively integrated. This integration requires a leader to be able to obtain the right amount—and also the right type—of information to continually monitor success. Great leaders don't simply rely on reports generated by department heads. Instead, they have an almost intuitive understanding of the company. By now you know that this intuition is actually the product of a deep understanding of the various stakeholders throughout the organization. Great leaders, and the NEOs reading this book, also understand the need to balance the satisfaction of these stakeholders.

Constantly shifting focus from one squeaky wheel to another can lead to confused employees, neglected customers, or unhappy owners. Conversely, balancing the needs of these three groups over time results in the best tool a leader can have: trust. When customers, employees, and owners know that their needs are always being considered, they're likely to support the company even when a particular program or initiative seems unappealing. People don't just want a leader who is popular, smart, or able to consistently reach quarterly profit goals. They want a leader they can trust.

THE IMPORTANCE OF BALANCE

This is the philosophical shift from focusing on satisfying CEOs to satisfying Cs, Es, and Os. Satisfying the CEO and meeting job expectations can offer good results for a while. You can take on a business problem, make it your own, succeed, and move on to the next project. This will get you recognized as a valuable manager, and it may even lead to salary increases or bonuses. But it won't help you develop the skills that will distinguish you from your peers. Practicing C.E.O. Satisfaction is the key to becoming a great leader.

In order to succeed in business, a manager must know how and when to employ a collection of strategies and skills. In order to succeed as a *leader*, a manager must be able to see, understand, and manipulate the interdependent needs of various key stakeholders. Clearly, senior leaders of organizations must possess this mind-set, but it's also important for junior executives, the future leaders, to adopt and practice it as they develop. The C.E.O. Satisfaction approach differentiates businesses but also differentiates individual people on a career track to become executive leaders.

WHO NEEDS BALANCE?

In business, balance means juggling the competing goals of many different departments, ensuring the right resources are being deployed at the right time, and keeping all of a company's moving parts aligned—all while maintaining focus on the overarching strategic vision. Businesses can be broken up into an infinite number of groups, but for the purposes of this book, we are using three: customers, employees, and owners.

Concentrating on satisfying each of these three key stakeholder groups should always be the focus of an effective leader. Leaders should not, therefore, spend time dividing each group into more complex sub-units. The C.E.O. Satisfaction approach requires two basic schools of thought: everyone fits into one of the three key stakeholder groups (customers, employees, and owners), and all of them are people who deserve to be understood, respected, and satisfied.

This isn't the only balancing act I'll address. That next one involves balancing your career objectives to accelerate your C.E.O. growth.

OPPOSITES BALANCE:
THE IDEA OF PARADOXICAL PAIRS

Much of the advice on how to accelerate your career and develop your executive skills focuses on excelling, performing, and producing. This type of advice is one dimensional, or output oriented. We've all attended lectures and read articles about how, in order to succeed, we must "over deliver." Or, we're told that in order to make sound business decisions, we must be objective at all times and resist being influenced by gut feelings: "if you can't measure it, you can't manage it," as the saying goes. And while we're talking about these "oldie-but-goodie" sayings, how many times have you been told about the power of action above all else? "Executives execute" and "it's all in the execution" are familiar phrases. My personal favorite is a bit of advice from the 1980s that championed the importance of learning by taking decisive action: It's not "ready, aim, fire," these advisors told us. It's "ready, fire, aim."

There's nothing wrong with these pieces of advice. They can help you develop your business skills, and there is a significant element of truth in each of them. But as I mentioned earlier, by staying focused solely on standard business expertise, managers risk remaining trapped in the forest, constantly managing new sets of trees. Successful leaders assess the quality of *inputs*, not just outputs, and consequently utilize a larger view: one that orchestrates these nuggets of wisdom with other insights and creative thinking to create balance. In this chapter, I use the concept of paradoxical pairs to illustrate the need to learn in a balanced, "both/and" approach rather than in one-dimensional, "either/or" way.

EXAMPLES OF PARADOXICAL PAIRS

I've already introduced the idea that a successful leader needs a unique combination of technical business expertise, people skills, and sound judgment. This combination is necessary to understand the interdependent and competing needs of different stakeholder groups, decide how to balance them in a way that keeps the business moving in the right direction, and constantly monitor and maintain a C.E.O. Satisfaction philosophy in a world of frequent and rapid change.

In the same way stakeholder groups pull the leader in

different tactical directions that have the potential to derail even the most carefully considered strategy, the leader's own set of skills and expertise can exert similar and conflicting pressures during key moments in every career. Remembering my commitment to solutions that take these differences into account in a way that is not "either or" but "both and," I offer a few examples of priorities that must be balanced in critical moments of managerial challenge. I believe that to be a steady-handed leader, a C.E.O. leader, an individual must develop these seemingly opposite skills in tandem. Most traditional feedback and reward systems favor the first part of these pairs, and if you pursue traditional feedback and reward, you'll develop that skill at the expense of its counter-skill. And probably at the expense of becoming a successful leader.

Facts and Feelings

Most people are taught that business is hard-nosed and objective. They learn to be motivated by risk mitigation and to back up all recommendations and decisions with facts. The more junior the employee and the more risk aversion in the corporate culture, the more formulaic a recommendation is likely to be. Because, after all, facts drive good business decisions; feelings have no place in this arena. That is, of course, unless you're one of the senior leaders, product geniuses, or sales superstars. They are allowed, and even expected, to use their gut feelings to help shape solutions. So where do their feelings come from? Most likely, years of experience, experience getting to know customers, employees, or owners, and having witnessed many decisions go either really well or totally miss the mark. The goal for NEOs is to use data to present a logical recommendation *and* to understand the feelings of the people impacted by recommendation. Results don't always turn out as planned because people are not as predictable as data is. If, while writing a recommendation, you can "put a face on it" and think about the people impacted by your decision, you can learn to develop your "feel." Experienced managers know that feel can be as important as facts in these situations. Here's an example to illustrate what I mean.

A major customer surprises your business with a threat of taking his business to a competitor. The customer suddenly doesn't like the terms of his contract. The potential loss of business is significant, so you call an emergency meeting with your management team and set a number of things in motion. The financial office determines the impact of various potential solutions, and legal counsel is asked to review a proposed change to the contract. Sales managers are asked to call the customer. They're also tasked with speaking to other customers—as discreetly as possible, of course—to see if there is something more to the story; maybe a competitor is actively trying to undercut the company in an attempt to steal clients. You might also try to determine if the customer's business is experiencing financial difficulties or undergoing change in ownership or management. All of this information will help frame your ultimate decision in a more complete way.

But even when all of this data is gathered and some of the mystery about what to do is addressed, you'll still need to make a final decision based in part on how you feel about the customer. There will always be considerations that cannot be evaluated with facts and numbers alone. For example, what if the customer is bluffing? If you grant his request for better contract terms, will he come back next year and demand even more? Is the customer a good partner? Do the two organizations have a history of reasonable negotiations? Ultimately, you'll have to decide if this is a customer the company wants to retain over the long term. Regardless of the answer, the details behind it are important.

How will your response to this challenge affect the company's other customers and its potential new customers? How will it change the company's position among its competitors? How will the company's suppliers and other allies respond? What might be the consequences of *those* actions? And, of course, you cannot ignore the two other stakeholder groups: the employees and owners. How will owners and employees view your response? Will they understand how it aligns with your overall strategy for success? Does that strategy suddenly seem too rigid and out of touch? Or, if you decide to alter the company's overall strategy in order to save this particular business relationship, how can you convince the owners and employees that you made the correct choice?

There's data to be gathered, of course, but not even the best data will yield a clear answer to complex challenges like this one. As a successful leader, you'll need to develop and use a "business feel." Common wisdom may tell us that this feel comes with years of experience. There's an element of truth in this, but time alone doesn't guarantee anything. Conversely, it's possible to develop a good feel quickly if you have the vision, imagination, and creativity to make every day a learning experience.

You can develop your business feel and learn to act quickly and decisively by implementing the CorePlus method. Don't worry—I'll go over this in more detail later on in the book.

Measurement and Messages

This paradoxical pair is about producing data to build a case versus building a narrative to produce a managerial initiative. Many junior employees think a good spreadsheet is all you need to convince people to follow your lead. But to be an effective leader, you also need to articulate the implications of the data. Stakeholders respond to more than data alone; they respond to the story a leader tells with the data. "Measurement and message" refers to the competing priorities of studying a situation before acting (measure) and communicating with key stakeholders (message).

There's an old business adage that I've heard time and time again. And every time I hear it, I question the leadership skills of the person saying it. The adage is "if you can't measure it, you can't manage it." Like most business concepts, this is a good one, and it's largely accurate. However, most of the people I've encountered who use this line are measurers—"build it and they will come" managers. They believe that if their reports say things are good, things are good—even if they're not.

I'm going to pick on telephone-based customer service models again. Over the last twenty-five to thirty years, telephone-based customer service has changed. Knowledgeable and accountable service people located close to their customers are becoming a thing of the past. Now, customer service representatives are consolidated in centralized processing centers and are often not in the same country as customers. Furthermore, telephone-based customer service models are often highly dependent on automated call management technology. During this evolution, call center expertise became more important than customer service expertise.

An entire business science has been developed around the use of sophisticated telephone technology—and that science is largely about measuring. As customer service became more consolidated and tech supported, call center managers began focusing primarily on metrics: calls per hour, average hold time, abandon rates, time to answer, and so forth. If you can measure it, you can manage it—and that's exactly what call centers did. "Time to talk" was the most vexing measurement. In large, consolidated call centers with hundreds or thousands of people, reducing the time spent on calls meant huge gains in efficiency. So call center "agents" (no longer called service representatives) were left with a challenge: should they spend a few extra minutes with a customer to ensure they've met their needs, or should they focus on keeping the call short in order to get a good review or bonus?

Call center managers collect data and call it "customer service metrics"—but really, it's productivity metrics. This is why the message priority is so important. What message do you want to send to your employees and customers? Ideally, you want your employees to be committed to providing customers with great service as efficiently as possible. However, when ninety-nine percent of the measuring is about productivity, not customer service, employees will understand what's truly important in their job performance. In this paradoxical pair, "message" refers to the experience a customer or employee has and how that experience matches what the company has promised to offer. The message needs to be clear, and the measurement should be designed around it.

As a developing C.E.O. Satisfaction leader, you'll likely be tasked with developing and assessing ways to measure a variety of projects, programs, and initiatives. Organizing and collecting data is important, but always remember to question the message behind it. Consider the message you're sending to employees, customers, and owners. In other words, put a face on it. Does the data you're measuring truly relate to the story you want to tell? I would guess that in most cases, measurements and messages are eighty to ninety percent aligned. The truly great leader will address the misalignment, however small it may be, and make adjustments accordingly.

Your message is important. Measurements are important.

Practice a "both/and" approach to measuring and messages as much as you can; the lessons will serve you well.

Deliver and Develop

This paradoxical pair reflects how you approach a business experience. Do you just try to get things done, or do you learn from them and help those around you learn from them as well? *Deliver* and *Develop* has to do with the higher value most cultures put on "delivering" or getting things done and the need to acquire, practice, and refine the skills and expertise of leadership ("develop"). Delivering is simply doing the job others have defined for you. Developing is creating the foundation for current and future leadership. Similar to the other pairs, the general belief in business is that both delivering and developing are critical. However, delivery, which is easily defined and measurable, often trumps development.

All of this ties in to a third concept, one I call the "expectations factor." The expectations factor relates closely to delivery. Many NEOs, particularly those in the early stages of their careers, believe that internalizing their job requirements and then over delivering on them will help advance their careers. This is the first expectations factor dilemma. Of course, over delivering can be a good thing. You can advance your career by exceeding expectations, which may, in turn, earn you a good reference from your boss. But sooner or later, doing things faster, cheaper, or in excess of targets will become less fruitful. Over delivering, by its very nature, means that someone else is in charge of measuring your success—not you. If the only value you got from your experience is that you were perceived as an over deliverer, you could be headed toward becoming a grinder or the specialist, not a leader.

A second expectations factor dilemma is related to the

quality of the projects you've been asked to execute. You may have delivered 130 percent of your sales quota or completed a project two weeks before the deadline, but a simple question remains: was this over delivering truly a result of your skills? You certainly want your achievements to be seen as proof of your unique and valuable skills; however, corporate leaders may believe at least part of your success was the result of inaccurate planning assumptions. And to be honest, they may not be entirely wrong about that in many cases. No matter how often an employee over delivers, there's still a question of how much he or she has actually achieved. Over delivery is not a solid foundation for becoming a leader.

The third expectations factor dilemma is perhaps the most important one: can an employee get caught in a cycle of over delivery? The ability to successful complete assignments is great, but until a manager demonstrates strategic aptitude by devising and implementing new initiatives, he or she may simply be assigned more and more projects. And I believe that executing more and more assignments for the same boss—or the same series of bosses—is not necessarily an opportunity to demonstrate leadership.

What's the solution for these expectation dilemmas? Create your own expectation factors, and don't rely solely on the expectations of your superiors. While your superiors may be interested in your development, assessing your delivery is often more important to them. So, with every assignment you take on, create your own personal development objectives: skills you want to strengthen, theories you'd like to test, and stakeholders you'd like to better understand. Make your development objectives as important as the delivery objectives. Later on, I'll discuss some practical advice to help you accomplish this.

Delivering is about doing, and developing is about thinking. In order to be a great leader, you need both. The thinking part is harder. So don't wait until you're finished doing to start learning how to think like a CEO.

Leading and Learning

This paradoxical pair reflects what type of leader you are: are you an infallible, independent decision maker, or are you willing to consider other opinions points of view? Tough, decisive leaders seem to be the most popular, and they have the reputation of having the ability to make hard decisions. There's a lot of truth in this. But without making learning a priority, the decisions a leader makes could be troublesome.

It gets to an issue similar to *Measure* and *Message*, but with the difference that, while "measure and message" applies in most cases to single challenges and opportunities as they arise during the course of business, "lead and learn" requires a more permanent commitment to a consistent managerial style. A leader committed to learning from key stakeholder groups must, by definition, be an excellent listener and is likely to be open to other people's ideas. That openness creates opportunities for building personal relationships, creating collaborative bonds, and establishing trust.

The good news is that when a NEO begins practicing the C.E.O. Satisfaction approach, he or she will most likely not have the knowledge and skills required to be an infallible, independent decision maker. NEOs need to learn, and they need to practice leading. Incorporating these two things into a single managerial style will help create a business culture that emphasizes listening to others, identifying the satisfiers of the three key stakeholder groups, and creating initiatives based on input from Cs, Es, and Os. Of all the paradoxical pairs introduced in this chapter, lead and learn is probably critical.

These four paradoxical pairs address different aspects of

business leadership. *Facts and Feel* relates to how decisions are made; *Measure and Message* relates to assessing performance and success; *Deliver and Develop* relates to your personal approach to how you work; and *Lead and Learn* relates to your leadership style. All eight words could be the title of a chapter in a management development curriculum, and generally, they are discussed independently. In addition, generally, the first word of each pair is given a higher value than the second. They're all equally important and interdependent.

I'll demonstrate later how the successful application of the CorePlus planning method can help you develop a consistent approach to all four paradoxical pairs. Remember, achieving a "both/and" balance for these pairs is a hallmark of true leadership. Resist the temptation to only pay attention to one half of these pairs, even though you may feel as if you're alienating your stakeholders. In fact, the opposite is true. Successfully finding and maintaining a balance that keeps the organization moving forward is something everyone—including the stakeholders—will notice. Practicing this aspect of the C.E.O. Satisfaction approach earns something far more valuable than any short-term returns: it earns trust.

BALANCE AND TRUST: WHERE IT ALL LEADS

The experience an NEO gains by navigating paradoxical pairs can improve his or her strategic agility and offers another learning opportunity: the ability to find balance. In this sense, my definition of balance is the ability to take in information that seems, or in fact, is, contradictory and to find an optimal solution that moves everyone forward without veering too much to the left or right in response to an individual challenge. Maintaining such a balance means first seeing potential misalignment, making a plan, and then executing it—sending a message, delivering a project, leading a team, and so on. When used together, the priorities described in the paradoxical pairs help maintain balance among an organization's stakeholder groups—and this, as you surely remember, is what a successful leader strives for.

Applying the C.E.O. Satisfaction methodology changed the way I looked at my jobs. Instead of following the directions of others (or more accurately, *in addition to* following these directions), I was able to lead. For me, leadership—the challenge of achieving success beyond expectations—was fun years ago, when it was more properly "core plus" planning, and it remains fun today. Practicing C.E.O. Satisfaction kept the boss happy in the early days of my career. And it keeps bosses happy today.

But today, that boss is me. I wish the same for you in your career, and I hope this book helps you achieve that.

CHAPTER 8

Becoming a C.E.O. Satisfier

YOU ARE HERE: LEARNING TO SATISFY THE PEOPLE IN YOUR SPHERE

As I mentioned earlier, my two aha moments came after I had already become a CEO. Still, these moments stemmed from the skills and strategies I had learned much earlier on in my career. These skills and strategies were the result of my interest in improving the satisfaction of my coworkers and our customers. Like the fictional Robert Hughes, I was able to create successful strategies for entire organizations because I had learned about the importance of satisfying stakeholders and viewing them as real people, maintaining balance, and earning trust. Because I took the time to understand my customers in Cincinnati well enough to know what they needed, I was able to keep them satisfied and my boss happy. Robert Hughes knew his customers well enough to understand their business models. He knew them as people, he learned how to satisfy them, and he earned their trust; in return, they taught him how to continue satisfying them as time went on. The same applies for Robert Hughes's approach to his company's employees and owners. He understood his industry, the markets, the employees, the investors, and the stockholders. Of course, he was no slacker when it came to studying the technical details of being a successful CEO, but he learned far more from his direct interactions with customers, employees, and owners. They, in return, learned that he was truly a man they could trust. Trust, of course, is the most valuable currency any leader can possess.

People often love to talk about what's important to them—and their general satisfaction is always important. Customers will tell you how they personally value your product or service, and they'll tell you about their businesses, too. Your colleagues are the same way. If you want to talk about quality with members of the manufacturing team, they'll be happy to oblige. People in the finance department might seem protective of information, but if you ask, they'll tell you what the critical performance indicators are and how your company is doing compared to them. My point here is that people are often a better source of information than books are. Furthermore, by talking to the people in the three stakeholder groups and working to align and balance their points of view, you can better learn to put a face on the issues you face at work. The earlier you learn that, the more successful you will be.

In summary, in order to practice C.E.O. Satisfaction, you need to be able to:

- Understand the satisfaction drivers of the key stakeholders
- Assess their current satisfaction levels
- Maintain alignment by constantly improving satisfaction without allowing a satisfier of one to become a dissatisfier for another

As you read the list above, you may have nodded your head in agreement despite still feeling like these are not things you can actively practice today—perhaps because of your junior role at work or your lower level job title. I firmly believe that no matter your current role, you can develop the C.E.O. Satisfaction skills that will set you apart from your colleagues throughout your career.

The C.E.O. practice program, which you can use to develop your C.E.O. skills, is based on two concepts: first, identifying your "spheres of influences" and second, employing CorePlus strategies within those spheres. *Spheres of influence* relate to connections with stakeholders or stakeholder satisfiers that your current role in the organization creates. You have two spheres, one created by where you sit in the organization structure and one created by your functional role within the organization. The following organizational charts provide a brief overview of how to view your spheres of influence and how you can utilize the different relationships you have with the people around you. Remember, your sphere might be larger than you think.

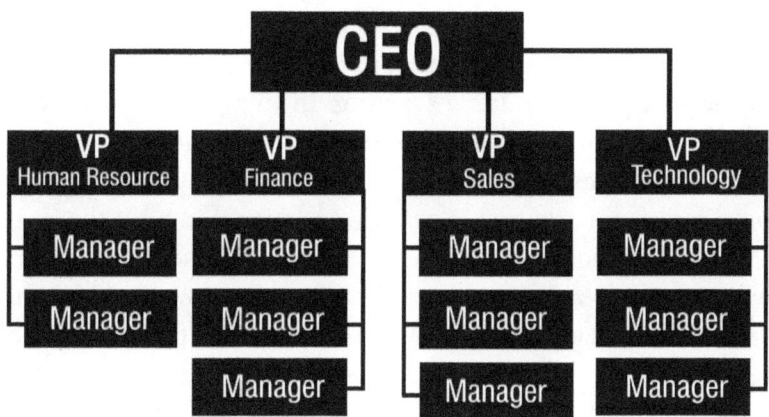

Figure 3

Let's begin our discussion with the figure on the previous page. It shows the classic "view from the top" of a generic corporate structure, with a CEO reporting to owners or a board of directors, and a series of managerial levels throughout the organization. Vice presidents report to the president/CEO; managers report to the VPs, and employees report to the managers. The CEO, highlighted in red, has most direct relationships with all three stakeholder groups. As I mentioned, the CEO has the classic "view from the top."

Within the company's structure, the CEO has only one kind of relationship with the employee stakeholders: He or she is superior to the vice presidents who are the CEO's direct reports and consequently, all other employees. There are no "equal" or peer relationships for a CEO. Yes, it's lonely at the top. Equal-impact relationships, which are available for all other members of a corporate staff, present opportunities for NEOs to develop their people skills and practice satisfying the customers, employees, and owners in their spheres of influence. To understand the point of view and the spheres of influence of an NEO, let's take a look at another chart.

In Figure 4, the NEO is the company's communications manager. He or she leads a team of three people and reports to the vice president for marketing. In this position, the NEO has is the opportunity to experience and manage three types of impact relationships: a subordinate relationship with the vice president for marketing, a superior relationship with the three communications staff members, and equal impact relationships with the other managers in the marketing department (in this case, the manager for customer relations and the manager of research).

These relationships make up the NEO's *organizational* sphere of influence. This sphere is a fertile laboratory in which the NEO can build his or her understanding of the employee

Organizational Sphere of Influence

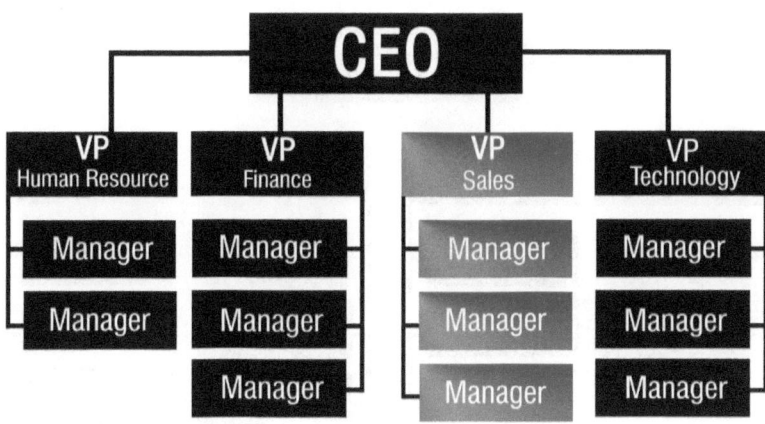

Figure 4

stakeholder group. In this example, you have an impact on your direct reports as their leader, you have an impact on your boss as his or her employee, and you have an impact on other managers as a peer and a teammate. These organizational sphere impact relationships are important because they provide direct and personal experience as a boss, peer, and employee. In your sphere, you'll experience real interpersonal communication as you make efforts to execute the company's objectives. For example, within your sphere of influence, you'll find that people will be less on guard, inputs will be direct and emotional, and results from improvement efforts will be visibly evident. During this time in your career, you can pick certain faces to etch in your mind; it's these faces that you'll recall later when considering the customers, employees, and owners.

If your organizational sphere provides a close-up opportunity to use impact relationships to develop Employee Satisfaction skills, what about customers and owners? In addition to your

Functional Sphere of Influence

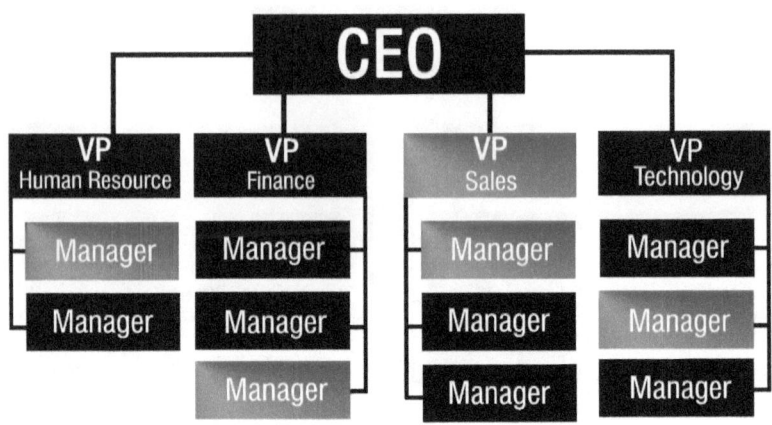

Figure 5

organizational sphere of influence, you also have a functional sphere of influence (see figure X). This is related to your functional role within the company and the impact opportunity afforded by that role. For example, a functional role in Sales or Marketing has an obvious impact on customers. But so does anything related to product/service operations and delivery or billing and collections. These functions have a direct impact on customers' perception of and satisfaction with the company. Similarly, corporate Finance should be closely aligned with the owner's satisfaction. But functions related to revenue (Pricing, Sales), gross margins (Purchasing), or expenses (everybody) all have impact relationship potential.

Once you map out your organizational and functional spheres, you'll likely find you have relationships that touch all three stakeholder groups. The organizational sphere and the functional sphere are places where a NEO can move freely in practicing the people skills and technical business expertise his or her career requires. Seek out experiences that will serve as "active learning opportunities"; I call them this because they allow for experimentation, and the resulting successes or failures are typically small enough to encourage risk taking. Within your spheres of influence, you can learn to keep your boss happy, and you can learn to be a good boss yourself. Your spheres provide you with a place to collaborate with your peers, and they're where you'll build your own CorePlus planning initiatives. Remember delivering on an assignment versus developing alignment? Your spheres of influence and your CorePlus initiatives will enable you to test your ability to create that alignment while simultaneously completing the assignment your boss has given to you—and completing them well!

Here is a different type of chart. You can use it to evaluate the people in your organizational sphere of influence. Thinking

Organizational Sphere

	Boss	Peer	Subordinate
Name			
Satisfaction 1-5			

Functional Sphere

	Customer	Employee	Owner
Name			
Impact			

Figure 6

about what satisfies them can help you structure your active learning experiences in a way that minimizes the risk of failure and increases the likelihood of success. The chart in Figure 6 is fairly straightforward, and it's certainly informal. Most importantly, however, it's for your eyes only; there's no need to share this information with anyone else, so be as honest as possible when filling it out. Look at each of the groups of people listed across the top of the chart. Write names down ("faces") under each category, and give each name a satisfaction rating on a scale from one to five, with one being barely engaged and five being highly motivated and enthusiastic about the company. Try to avoid using threes—that's a bit of a copout. Force yourself to put them on the positive or negative side of the scale. If you're unable to provide a rating, you have a great learning opportunity. The important part of this exercise is to think about the needs and satisfiers of the people in your immediate sphere of influence.

The other part of the chart pertains to your functional sphere of influence. Each of the three stakeholder groups—customers, employees, and owners—are listed in a vertical column. Next to each group, jot down the various ways your functional role can impact that stakeholder. They don't need to have huge impacts, and they don't need to be fully fleshed out. Focus on things you could potentially do rather than on things you've done. If it helps, go back and review the chapters that discuss satisfying each group. Again, this chart is for your eyes only. It will be useful as we begin our discussion of putting ideas into action with CorePlus planning.

COREPLUS PLANNING: THE WAY TO DEVELOP YOUR OWN BUSINESS FEEL

Some leaders appear to make decisions almost instinctively. But it's not really instinct if the leader's actions are based on a sound understanding of the context in which a challenge might develop. It's what I described earlier as strategic agility, and it's something that can be learned, practiced, and perfected. From the first chapter of this book, I've advocated establishing personal goals for yourself that are separate from the ones required by your job title. Doing this is the key first step in developing a larger set of business expertise. This approach, which I've introduced a few times as CorePlus planning, is a way for you to move beyond keeping the boss happy, checking off boxes on assignments, and always thinking about your next annual performance review. CorePlus planning is really no more complicated than practicing the full C.E.O. Satisfaction methodology within your current sphere of influence. It means looking to the key stakeholder groups in your organization and personally creating plans to satisfy them. This is good practice not only because it helps you develop problem-solving skills, but it also accelerates your understanding of the stakeholders as people. At the beginning of the book I mentioned that C.E.O. Satisfaction is based on assessing, aligning, and achieving. This is the achieving part.

With enough practice, you'll learn how to satisfy the key stakeholder groups while also maintaining your vision as a leader. You'll find that your deliberate efforts to maintain a CorePlus planning approach will gradually form that gut instinct great leaders seem to have. And one day, you may just earn enough trust to become a CEO.

There are a few important guidelines for making CorePlus planning work for you.

1. Incorporate quarterly milestones into your annual plans

This is a model that requires you to be committed to your goals. By writing down your objectives and assessing your progress every quarter, you can train yourself to keep the needs of all three stakeholder groups in mind on a regular basis. Think about a long-term challenge you've taken on: losing ten pounds by summer, graduating in four years, or saving up to buy a house by your thirtieth birthday. In every case, there's a timeline of specific actions you'll need to take if you want to achieve your goal on time. Consider CorePlus your plan for becoming a president, CEO, or executive leader within a certain number of years. To accomplish that goal, you'll need to hit several milestones along the way.

2. Take small steps in CorePlus to achieve big leaps in strategic agility

Depending on your experience and your spheres of influence, mastering C.E.O. Satisfaction may take three years, or it make take ten. In any case, don't try to swallow it whole. Instead, take small bites. Remember, the objective of this approach is to understand the things that satisfy customers, employees, and owners—both as stakeholders and as humans. So, plan small initiatives that involve only a few people; this will help you succeed over time and will enable you to build to bigger initiatives as your skill set grows. Set achievable goals to get the most out of your experiences.

3. You're the Boss of CorePlus.

This is very important. *You* set the CorePlus plans and objectives, and *you* assess your results and progress. Nearly all the time at work, someone else determines what your projects will be and how well you executed them. Not here. You create goals for yourself, and you hold yourself accountable for achieving them. This will take some extra work, and at times you might find it challenging. But here's the reality: if you can't effectively be your own boss, you can't be someone else's.

In its simplest terms, CorePlus works in tandem with C.E.O. methodology to address the concerns of customers, employees, and owners. Companies frequently use some sort of performance assessment tool for employees. The items on this assessment tool represent the contract between you and your boss, and it's important to meet performance standards. CorePlus is a separate plan or "contract" you set for yourself. It includes any objectives from your boss's "contract" that address customer, employee, or owner satisfaction—the Core. In addition, it ensures that every quarter you are working on satisfying all three stakeholders by adding your personal objectives to your boss's objectives—the Plus. The Plus objectives can be actual initiatives or targeted learning opportunities.

This is what it looks like:

Quarterly Goal			
	Customer Satisfaction	Employee Satisfaction	Owner Satisfaction
Core Objective			
Plus Objective			
Learning Objective			

Figure 7

First, under "Core Objective," fill in anything from your boss's expectations that directly or indirectly affects the satisfaction of each stakeholder. Nearly every job in the company hits one, maybe two of these; however, it may not have been evident until you put it through a C.E.O. filter. Next, write down your learning objectives. Use the "Learning Objective" to help understand how your Core objectives really impact stakeholder satisfaction. For example, let's say your core objective is to update your company's software to meet the requirements set by the product management team. The team needs you to make the changes in order to improve the customer experience. If you're only focused on satisfying your boss, you'll then you execute your duties and deliver the project. However, if you practice C.E.O. Satisfaction, you'll also make an effort to learn how and why the changes improve the customer experience. In doing so, you might find that you disagree with the requirements laid out by your bosses. The goal is not to challenge your organization; the goal is to learn, observe, and draw your own conclusions. Once you complete your project, your next objective to assess its impact.

Example A

Matt runs a customer service operation that includes a call center function with roughly 100 employees. In this function, there is an intake role, fulfillment role, and report role. In his Core quarterly objectives, Matt is expected to improve the accessibility for customers and final delivery (Customer Satisfaction) while also hitting productivity improvement targets (Owner Satisfaction). The only formal requirement for Employee Satisfaction is putting development plans in place for his future supervisors. A challenging set of goals on top of the everyday challenge of keeping the operation running. But Matt wants to be a CEO Sat leader so he has challenged himself with a few additional goals. Under Customer Satisfaction, he understands that intake errors creates delays or redos that impacts overall customer experience so he will examine causes and improve processes. And by spending time to help his supervisors really understand who their customers are, they will be better at independent decision making. Under Employee Satisfaction, he is focusing on one individual this quarter who may be a Grinder or Solid Citizen but Matt believes there is more potential. Finally, he'll contribute to Owner Satisfaction by preparing his leaders to carry a bigger load in anticipation of needing further productivity contributions.

Service Operations Mgr

	Customer Satisfaction	Employee Satisfaction	Owner Satisfaction
Core Objectives	1. Improve answer time to 85% of calls within 20 sec 2. Deliver final reports to customers within 2 days of appointment	1. Complete development plans for all team leaders	1. Achieve planned productivity increase for quarter 2. Negotiate improved telephone rates
Plus Objectives	1. Decrease intake errors; find root cause 2. Teach unit supervisors the profiles of top ten clients	1. Assist Joseph to pass supervisor aptitude test	1. Train managers to handle a higher supervisor: staff ratio

Figure 8

Example B

Paula manages a team of 8 people who are responsible for the retention and product penetration of 10 large national customers. Her formal or CORE objectives are generally being assigned to her. Under Customer Satisfaction, she has some critical implementations that have been committed to customers and under Employee Satisfaction, she has to execute on a few programs assigned by HR and IT. Her Owner Satisfaction goals are also assigned to her as goals to increase pricing and push some new products. She also has her own goals, some aggressive Plus goals. She will deepen her understanding of her customer's satisfaction drivers by becoming an active support system as her customer prepares for a critical presentation. Paula has a new and inexperienced employee with great potential and with focus on helping that employee break through on presentation skills while helping the entire team understand the levers of their incentive compensation model. And while collections is largely a back room operation, she would like to better understand cash flow so Paula sets a goal to directly work on the receivables of one or two of her clients as a learning opportunity.

Manager of Account Mgt

	Customer Satisfaction	**Employee Satisfaction**	**Owner Satisfaction**
Core Objectives	1. Implement new reporting package for customer X and Y 2. Ensure special instructions for customer Z are implemented accurately	1. Complete interim appraisals for 4 team members 2. Provide training on new applications to support staff	1. Implement price increases to customer A and B 2. Sell new products to 3 customers
Plus Objectives	1. Assist contact at customer V to present program results to their board	1. Help Jane with presentation ability 2. Ensure all staff fully understands their commission/bonus programs	1. Work with clients with worst receivables to identify logjams

Figure 9

Example C

Bill and his team have fairly focused assigned quarterly objectives that only include Employee Satisfaction and Owner Satisfaction because his manager is not a CEO Sat leader and only focuses on his/her assigned goals. But Bill wants more so he will set goals to meet directly with a few customers to observe the interactions and learn more about how they succeed in their jobs. He also recognizes that the nature of his team's project work often translates into very long days and even weekends in the effort to support their department's need for information and this puts stress on his staff. By proactively engaging his team to develop a model that eases this demand, he'll learn more about the individual motivators for his team. Finally, even though he's not been tasked with this project, he has noted an unusually high cancellation rate of a product. For his own education, he'll apply his analysis skills to help root out a cause which may help his company fix the product or plan for its shortfall.

Financial Analysis Director

	Customer Satisfaction	Employee Satisfaction	Owner Satisfaction
Core Objectives		1. Upgrade tools and training for team 2. Provide performance feedback	1. Develop new pricing model for product X 2. Determine causes of slow receivable performance from mid-market
Plus Objectives	1. Visit clients with Sales team to learn how they make purchase decisions	1. Work with team to develop solutions for work/life balance	1. Work with Sales team to minimize early cancellations of product Y

Figure 10

There are an infinite number of ways to increase satisfaction in your organizational and functional spheres of influence. Consider the employees in your spheres of influence. Are they grinders? Solid citizens? Are they satisfied and engaged? If not, what can you do to improve their satisfaction? At the very least, try to understand the roots of the dissatisfaction. Quite honestly, just the process of finding all the connections described in C.E.O. Satisfaction puts you on a path toward enlightened leadership. The objective is to systematically and thoughtfully explore the satisfiers of each stakeholder group while keeping all stakeholders aligned. Doing this in small ways early on in your career will help you always consider the Customer Satisfaction, Employee Satisfaction, and Owner Satisfaction on a personal level later on.

Final Thoughts

My goal in the first eight chapters was to introduce my leadership philosophy, to teach you the CEO Satisfaction approach, and to show you how to adopt these concepts and use them to enhance your career.

The CEO Satisfaction approach begins as you balance the interests of the three key business stakeholders, takes flight as you recognize the satisfaction drivers for each stakeholder, and soars as you create actionable techniques that continually hone your skills. If you adopt this philosophy and introduce these techniques, you may one day be in the position of the fictional Robert Hughes from the opening chapter, looking back on a successful career, reminiscing about your accomplishments.

I had that personal experience when I retired from a company I led for ten years.

At my retirement dinner, speakers gently roasted me before generously thanking me. Most focused on aspects of our business success during my tenure – revenue and profit growth, mergers and acquisitions, new businesses launches. When it was my turn at the podium, I reflected on some of the same topics but in a very different way. When I recalled those achievements, I didn't discuss them merely in terms of numbers, percentages, and sales goals. I evoked the "faces" I worked with to achieve those things.

Throughout this book, I have urged you to "put a face on it." Business achievements are the result of people from all stakeholder groups making decisions and acting upon them; my achievements, in my mind, are summed up in a collection of faces, and thinking of them that way makes those achievements even more fulfilling.

For example, there's Amelia, who was a $15 hourly entry level employee when we first met. Through her own drive, and fueled by the company's interest in developing talent, Amanda became a supervisor, then a project leader, and then a manager. During this period, she also completed an MBA and tripled her income level.

She was one of many "untapped potential" individuals I have worked with during my career.

There's Jason, the Private Equity partner who owned a majority of our business. In the first two years of our relationship, the company could have generated much higher profitability, had that been our only goal. But he supported making strategic investments in our operating platform as we created new products and hired key people. The result: our business grew significantly through organic growth and acquisitions, resulting in a tremendous return for the ownership.

A very early customer, Leon, was willing to partner with me as we created an improved delivery model for his company. He could have simply requested proposals from our competitors and selected the cheapest option. Instead, he helped me understand why certain capabilities were critical to achieving his business goals. Once we delivered on those needs, we were awarded the balance of Leon's business, and our model became a template to bring to other clients.

I could write an entire book describing my experiences with

Customer "faces," Employee "faces," and Owner "faces." Some of those faces may have intersected with my journey for only a split second, and some have become lifelong friends, but all have had a positive and lasting impact on me. Following the CEO Satisfaction approach will make you a better business leader and can lead to MORE business success and financial reward. The big payoff, however, is the ability to amass a collection of mutually satisfying experiences with the people you encounter as you create that business success. If you can do that, then you will not only have business success, but you will also have a very fulfilling career. You will have not only satisfied your Customers, your Employees, and your Owners – you will have satisfied yourself.

I hope this book helps you achieve that business and personal success!

www.ingramcontent.com/pod-product-compliance
Lightning Source LLC
Chambersburg PA
CBHW020921180526
45163CB00007B/2834